KEEP ON PEDALING

KEEP ON PEDALING

The Complete Guide to Adult BICYCLING

NORMAN D. FORD

The Countryman Press

WOODSTOCK, VERMONT

FIRST EDITION

Copyright © 1990 by Norman D. Ford

All rights reserved. No part of this book may be reproduced in any form or by any electronic or mechanical means including information storage and retrieval systems without permission in writing from the publisher, except by a reviewer who may quote brief passages.

Library of Congress Cataloging-in-Publication Data

Ford, Norman D., 1921–
    Keep on pedaling: the complete guide to adult bicycling/
Norman D. Ford. — 1st ed.
        p.   cm.
    ISBN 0-88150-154-9
    1. Cycling.   2. Bicycle touring.   3. Middle age.   I. Title.
GV1041.F66   1990
    796.6'4 — dc20   89-37057
                                                          CIP

Design by James F. Brisson
Illustrations copyright © by Patricia Witten
Cover photograph by Carolyn L. Bates (fStop Pictures, Inc.)

Printed in the United States of America

2   3   4   5   6   7   8   9   10

*To my wife, Shirley,
who used the advice in this book
to take up recreational bicycling
at age 50.*

ACKNOWLEDGEMENTS

Among the scores of veteran bicyclists and others who helped make this book possible, I would especially like to thank Katharine Parker, editor; Greg Siple of Bikecentennial; Jean and Hartley Alley of Boulder, Colorado; Toby B. Pyle of American Youth Hostels; David B. Rusling, Tour Manager of Backcountry Bicycle Tours; W. David Walls, Publishing Director of *Velo News*; Anne Parish of Backroads Bicycle Touring; Arlene Plevin, Editor of the League of American Wheelmen's *Bicycle USA*; Bill Perry, Director, Vermont Bicycle Touring; Diane Fritschner, Editor of U.S. Cycling Federation's *Cycling U.S.A.*; Frank Behrendt of International Bicycling Tours; Ruth and Bob Husky, indefatigable tandem tourists of Lake Worth, Florida; and Holly Gems, Program Assistant, Bicycle Institute of America. I owe a special debt of gratitude to Richard Mauldin of Bicycles Etcetera Bicycle Shop, Kerrville, Texas, who guided me through the intricacies of bicycle mechanics; and to my editor at Countryman Press, Carl Taylor, a wordsmith *par excellence*, whose continued patience and support made this book possible.

Norman D. Ford

The publisher also gratefully acknowledges the assistance of the many people who helped generously in the creation of this book, especially: Howard Stone, author and bicycle touring expert; Marilee Attley, racing expert, of Vitesse Press, Brattleboro, Vermont;

Jane Grey North of Community Nutrition Services, Hartford, Vermont; Dr. Min Aung, orthopedic surgeon of Dallas, Texas; Randy Koetsier of The Cyclery Plus, Woodstock, Vermont; and Richard Wallace of Omer's and Bob's Cyclery, Hanover, New Hampshire.

Needless to say, none of the persons acknowledged bears any responsibility for the final text of the book, for which the author and publisher are fully responsible.

CONTENTS

By using lower, easy-to-pedal gears, riders as old as 79 have cycled the length of the world's highest paved road to the 14,267-foot summit of Colorado's Mount Evans.

CHAPTER 1

The New Fitness—Why Adult
Bicycling Is "In" Today

- You've just received a letter from a friend five years older than you, ecstatically describing a bicycle tour she recently took through the Soviet Union.
- Another friend, ten years your senior, calls to say he has finally found the ideal competitive sport. "It's bicycle racing," he says. "It's impact-free but full of excitement and challenge."
- You read about a 65-year-old man who explores abandoned Rocky Mountain railroad beds on a sturdy, fat-tired bicycle especially designed for off-road mountain travel.

*I*f you're a mature adult and live in our modern fitness culture, you have undoubtedly heard equally alluring stories about bicyclists who are often years older than you. It usually doesn't take many of these glowing accounts to persuade you that—despite your age—bicycling can open up exciting new horizons of fitness, fun, and travel. In fact, you probably have already considered the wisdom of taking up bicycling.

Yet you hesitate because you realize that bicycling isn't all pluses. You probably recall acquaintances who started into bicycling after reaching the 30–40-year age bracket. Chances are that most stashed away their bicycles in the garage a few days or weeks after beginning, and those bicycles are still there.

In short, about three out of every four mature Americans who attempt to take up bicycling fail to stay with it. Only the exceptional man or woman seems to really catch bicycle fever and to go on and succeed.

1

It's an admitted fact that many adult Americans fail to stay with most types of exercise. But lack of fitness is not, I discovered, the reason for the high dropout rate among adult bicyclists. The greatest barrier for most adults is psychological: fear of failing or of looking silly, plus feeling intimidated by lack of know-how.

The majority of adult newcomers to cycling are so unaware of the basics that most never really experience sports bicycling at all. Too often older adults innocently buy youngsters' bicycles in the fond belief that one 12-speed is the same as another. The result is that they give up without ever experiencing the joy and exhilaration of riding a high-performance bicycle.

Even owning a quality bicycle does not guarantee success. Most bikes you see in top-category bike shops are designed and built for people under 25 years of age, and they are usually sold by people under 40, few of whom have any idea of the special needs and problems of mature bikers. Bicycle salespeople are just beginning to learn of the varied options available to enhance the performance of older riders such as installing lower gears or longer crankarms.

Taking Up Bicycling Later in Life

For these and many other reasons, I'm convinced that men and women who take up bicycling in adulthood need a totally different introduction to the sport.

Although this book was originally intended for those taking up bicycling in mid-life (ages 40–65) it quickly became apparent that the same guidance can benefit adults of any age who are moderately active but not athletic.

If you can jump on an all-terrain or road bike and go blasting up a mountain road, you probably don't need this book. But if you'd like to ride up hills or to ride long distances without tiring, but you can't at present, then this book is for you regardless of age.

So my purpose in this book is to provide the guidance, information, and advice to help you break into bicycling successfully, and to emphasize the many exciting ways in which you can enjoy your bike.

Good Health Is the Only Requirement

If you biked when you were younger, and are in generally good condition and free of physical defects, recreational bicycling is an easy sport to get back into. That's exactly what Ed Delano of Davis,

California, discovered back in the sixties. After not having ridden for 39 years, he began bicycling again at age 58.

Ed soon became so hooked on bicycling that he took up both racing and touring. Among the many tours he has made are four solo rides across America, including a fabulous 34-day trip from Vacaville, California, to Quebec City, Canada, made when he was 70.

Even in his 80s Ed continues to ride competitively and in 1987 he won three gold medals at the U.S. National Senior Olympics. All through the years, bicycling has kept him in better shape than most men half his age.

For proof, when he was tested recently at the University of Florida Center for Exercise Fitness, Ed's oxygen uptake was double that for the average man his age. In fact, his aerobic capacity exceeded the "very good" category for men in their 20s, and was 30 percent better than that of most runners of his age.

Like Ed Delano, millions of adults have turned back the aging clock through bicycling regularly. Several studies have shown that bicycle racers have the highest oxygen uptake, and a greater ability to deliver oxygen to the muscles, than athletes in any other sport. Other studies have confirmed that sports bicycling provides health and fitness benefits equal to or greater than those of running or swimming.

The Nonimpact Sport

These facts have sent converts from aerobic dancing and jogging flocking into bicycling because of its freedom from impact. Pedaling at a brisk pace minimizes pressure on ankles, knees, and hips and makes joint injuries extremely rare. In fact, you can continue to bicycle until very late in life with minimal risk of injury or of tearing down the body.

Yet bicycling uses all the main muscle groups, creating long, lean muscles and a firm, athletic build. Riding stationary bicycles is the most frequently prescribed exercise at cardiac rehabilitation centers. Bicycling is also a superb way to lose weight. Pedaling briskly at 15 m.p.h., a 120-pound woman burns 402 calories per hour while a 150-pound man burns 504.

However, these and other benefits accrue only to those who pedal at a brisk enough pace. That means spinning the pedals at a cadence of 60–90 r.p.m. or more. (Cadence is the cyclist's term for revolutions per minute.) To anyone taking up bicycling after age 25, this fact is of paramount importance. It defines the difference between "casual" bicycling and "sports" or "recreational" bicycling.

There are two ways to bicycle:

• *Casual bicycling* implies riding on bicycle paths or in parks or around the neighborhood, usually on a 3-, 5-, or 12-speed bicycle purchased in a department store and intended for youngsters. Casual bikers travel at a relatively slow pace, often on flat terrain. They ride infrequently, usually on calm, sunny days, and *they pedal at a cadence of less than 60 r.p.m.* Also known as neighborhood bicycling, or once-around-the-park riding, casual bicycling offers relatively few weight loss or fitness benefits, and most casual riders have a low fitness level. They seldom travel more than ten or fifteen miles on a ride.

• *Sports or recreational bicycling* means riding regularly on the open road using a high-performance, multigeared bicycle with a range of gears wide enough to match the changing terrain. **This means that a pedal cadence of 60–90 r.p.m. or more can be maintained almost constantly.** Sports bicyclists are more dedicated. They ride up and down hills and may even ride through off-road terrain. They seldom ride for less than 15 miles, and many older adults are capable of covering up to 75 miles or more in a day.

While the terms *sports* and *recreational* bicycling are often used interchangeably, strictly speaking sports bicycling refers to riding a sports or racing bicycle for fitness training or competition. Recreational bicycling usually refers to riding a touring or mountain bike for day rides or longer tours.

But since the definitions of sports and recreational bicycling frequently overlap, the term sports bicycling as used in this book frequently embraces both sports and recreational bicycling.

Casual bicycling is such a dead-end pursuit that I'm going to lay it to rest right now. If you're into casual bicycling already, this book can help you move up to sports bicycling as smoothly and as swiftly as possible.

Sports Bicycling—Fitness Plus Adventure

The rest of this book is about breaking into sports bicycling. Owning a high-performance bicycle can open up a whole new world of fun, fitness, travel, and even competition. Among all modes of exercise, bicycling covers more ground in less time with a minimum of effort. You can exercise while exploring local country roads, or you can sign up for organized bike tours that take you roaming the backroads of Europe, the United States, Nepal, or New Zealand. You don't have to camp out or sleep in a hostel. Over 100 tour operators provide scenic tours of 5–14 days or more with comfortable overnight accommodations in cozy inns or luxurious lodges, and with fine dining in gourmet restaurants. While you're riding, a van carries your baggage and picks up any stragglers.

Alternatively, you can tour the United States, Europe, or New Zealand on your own, staying overnight and eating at the same hotels, motels, and restaurants you would patronize if you were traveling by car.

With a mountain bike you can explore traffic-free old mining roads, railroad beds, and even some trails high in the Rockies or in scores of national forests and state or national parks. Organized tours are available for mountain bikers too.

If you like to ride with groups, almost every city now has a bicycle club. And there are rallies, festivals, and group rides all over the country where you can meet and ride with hundreds of other bicyclists. Single men and women often meet future mates on these rides or while on tours.

Almost any moderately fit adult between 25 and 65 or older can take up sports bicycling. You don't have to be an athlete, nor do you have to be young; and you don't need any prior experience beyond the ability to ride a bicycle.

The Health Benefits of Bicycling

Sports bicycling, when done on a regular basis, builds exceptional stamina and energy, and most people who bike regularly seldom feel tired or fatigued. Studies have shown that bicycling regularly lessens depression, stress, and anxiety; increases sexual vigor; lowers blood pressure; improves sleep; and improves almost all risk factors for heart disease and stroke. Active people in good physical condition have a longer life expectancy than those who are sedentary and out of shape, and are less susceptible to cancer and other diseases. And the brisk pace of sports bicycling releases endorphin in the brain, which often brings on a feeling of euphoria.

Bicycling regularly can also give you a feeling of mastery and control over your life and health. Finding yourself riding farther and faster each time boosts your self-esteem and creates a powerful feeling of success and achievement.

Naturally, all these benefits are available to women as well as men. Actually, more women than men are now buying road bikes and race categories exist for women at local and national racing levels up to age 70. In fact, older women are excelling in racing.

At age 67, Margareta Lambert of Dillon, Colorado, won three gold medals in the 1987 Senior Olympics. And Genny Mayberry was 45 before she took up competitive bicycling. Competing first at local time trials, then at Masters District races, and finally at the national level, by age 51 she had become National Masters Champion 5 years in a row. Another superb adult woman athlete is Casey Patterson, a 43-year-old mother of three, who showed it is never too late to take up bicycling by winning the 1987 Race Across AMerica.

Older newcomers, both men and women, can excel in bicycle racing in just a brief time. Through the Masters racing program — which begins at age 30 — you can compete with men and women in your own age group, and go on to compete at a national event. Because it's a noninjurious sport that can be continued for a lifetime, men and women in their 70s and 80s are still able to compete and win.

When Are You Too Old to Bicycle?

If you still think you're too old to take up bicycling, you should know that bicycle touring is dominated by men and women in the 40–70 year age range, and some are even older. Says David B. Rusling, tour manager of Backcountry Tours: "We get many guests on our tours who are well over forty and, surprisingly, much of the time they are the stronger riders."

Even on American Youth Hostels tours many participants are well over 40, and bikers in their 70s have ridden on American Youth Hostels' tours of New Zealand.

The same trends are echoed by Frank Behrendt, president of International Bicycle Tours, who told me: "Over half the riders on our tours are aged sixty and over, largely because they have the time and money to afford our longer bike tours to Europe and the U.S.S.R." Frank added that IBT had taken literally hundreds of bicyclists aged 60 and over and he could not recall one who was unable to make the distance or who ran out of energy.

Another expert, Greg Siple, art director of Bikecentennial (a national bicycle touring association and route information service), also points out that bicycling is no longer just for the young.

Quoting statistics from the annual two-day Tour of the Scioto River Valley, which drew 6,100 riders in 1988, Greg emphasizes that nearly 29 percent were aged 40 or over. Back in the sixties, a majority of the TOSRV riders were under 25. In 1988, however, the majority of riders were aged 28–38.

Confirming the growth of adult bicycling is the fact that over 850,000 American adults took a bicycle-touring vacation in 1988. Over 1.7 million adult bicyclists ride at least once each week; over 5 million adults own a mountain bike. Today adult bicycling is enjoying its greatest resurgence since the 1880s. The main reasons are disillusionment with the automobile, frustration with high-impact sports like jogging and aerobics, and development of the modern high-performance bike.

Today's Bicycles Are User-Friendly

If you haven't ridden a bicycle in several years, you're in for some pleasant surprises. Fumbling for the right gear or having to walk uphill is now just a memory. Futuristic-looking bikes are appearing that are so astonishingly light and fast that models built only a few years ago seem like antiques by comparison. In fact, today's medium-priced bikes are superior to top-of-the-line models of five or six years ago. Today, for a few hundred dollars you can ride a bike equal in quality to one that a few years ago might have been ridden in the Tour de France.

Indexed gear shifters click you into exactly the right gear setting while aerodesign brake levers eliminate the cable housing formerly looped over the handlebars. Toeclips and straps have given way to step-in pedals that lock your shoe to the pedal but release like ski bindings. Meanwhile, energy efficient, elliptical chainrings are as standard on modern bikes as the steep frame angles and short wheelbases that provide an astonishingly fast and responsive ride. (Chainrings are the toothed wheels near the pedals, while the wheelbase is the distance between the front and rear axles.)

Handlebar computers measure speed and distance, and the more sophisticated models may also display your pedal cadence, your pulse rate, and even the total elevation gain of all the hills that you have climbed on your ride.

Nor need you ride in the crouched-over racing position. Sit astride a contemporary mountain bike and you'll discover you're in the familiar upright position with a comfortable cushioned saddle, with fat tires that swallow bumps, and with cantilever brakes so powerful that you can stop on the proverbial dime.

You're at the controls of one of the most energy-efficient vehicles ever designed for overland travel. From calories in food its human rider can deliver more net power to the road than can any car from its gasoline fuel.

At the flick of a thumb you command an astonishing range of 12 to 21 speeds, or even more, from low, hill-gobbling gears that can also slice through headwinds, to big gears that can take you cruising downhill at 40 m.p.h. While you spin the pedals at 60–90 r.p.m. the multiple gearing smooths out rough roads and hills. Today's bikes offer unprecedented efficiency, comfort, safety, speed, and handling ability.

Your mountain bike can take you up narrow trails, or on slick-rock, to remote places where two wheels may never have gone before. You can ride across streams or shallow rivers and go anywhere that a four-wheel drive vehicle or trail bike can venture. Your go-anywhere bike is equally at home on the highway, and it can cross congested cities faster than most cars. At nominal cost you can put it on a plane and fly it to Europe or New Zealand and ride it out of the airport for a month-long tour. Or you can mount your bike on an indoor trainer and make it double as an exercise bike.

You can park your bike where there is no parking space for cars, or stop and admire the view anywhere at any time. Burning only excess calories and cholesterol, it gives you total freedom from the gasoline pump. Your bike is quiet, nonpolluting, and nonlethal. It seldom breaks down. It requires no hefty insurance premiums. And it costs roughly one-twentieth as much as a new automobile.

Explore the World by Pedal Power

The sheer joy of riding a modern high-performance bike has become the focus of the growing trend toward active, outdoor adventure vacations. Millions of middle-class Americans today are bored with cars, golf, and crowded beaches and are seeking more active and challenging vacations.

Bicycle touring supplies both fitness and adventure in a single package, tour operators have discovered. When cozy lodgings and great food are added, the combination is irresistible.

Not long ago I sampled a bike tour through New England operated by one of the largest bike tour firms. With a dozen other adults

I rode on secluded backroads through a Rip Van Winkle world of white farms, villages, and maple sugar houses that seemed to have slumbered since the 1930s. One afternoon we coasted downhill for miles beside the foaming Ammonoosuc River before plunging through a century-old covered bridge to the historic inn where we were to spend the night.

Each evening we had ample time for a relaxing soak in a hot tub bath before joining the rest of our group around the lounge fire for a glass of apple cider. Everyone seemed to have some special adventure to relate, from discovering bits of old horses' harness in a farmer's barn to being invited into the home of a New England conservationist for afternoon tea.

Brisk outdoor exercise by day, country inns and homecooked meals at night. If that sounds like the kind of adventure vacation you'd prefer, consider a bicycle tour. All over America, fitness-minded adults are trading four wheels for two and discovering a new type of vacation based on good food, camaraderie, and fitness-building adventure.

There are tours galore for cycling purists, or you can choose from luxury trips that combine mountain bicycling with skiing or trekking, or bicycle touring with hot air ballooning or a schooner cruise.

Motoring Isn't Fun Any More

But the most potent driving force behind the mushrooming growth of bicycle touring, and other active outdoor vacations, is total disgust and disenchantment with the automobile. No longer is there any pleasure in driving a car. Stress and tension are your reward for driving on freeways and most other major roads. Even on lesser roads you must maintain the hectic pace of other traffic or be honked at. Only in remote areas is it still possible to shunpike on deserted roads. Elsewhere, driving translates into traffic gridlock and smog amid an endless look-alike world of minimarkets, fast-food outlets, and chain motels.

Compared to the magnificent freedom of bicycle touring, the countryside is just a blur to passing motorists while the driver sees only the road and the cars ahead. Totally isolated from the outdoors, deprived of all movement, and cut off from all contact with the region they are passing through, automobile tourists get only the most superficial impression of where they have been. Often, parking is available only at fast-food restaurants and tourist traps.

Although they are forced to own cars, most bicyclists have learned to spend as little time as possible inside them. For vacations, at least, bicycles are rapidly becoming a viable alternative to the polluting a id environmentally destructive automobile.

Serendipity Galore

By comparison, a bicycle is a true vehicle for personal discovery. Whether at a country store or during a café stop, a modern bike makes a wonderful conversation piece that often leads to encounters with local people or with the foods, wines, or other cultural features of a region. Roaming through New England, we've more than once stumbled on a firemen's benefit offering huge platters of steaming lobster, and in Guatemala we were invited to join a wedding reception.

In Indonesia or Nepal you travel as the people do, bicycling along with hundreds of locals and meeting them face to face. The serendipity and adventure of bicycle touring so expands one's travel horizons that once having taken a bicycle tour, few adults are ever again willing to accept the restrictions of automobile travel.

Although they buy their bicycles primarily to lose weight, lower blood pressure, or to knock points off their cholesterol, most adults soon discover that owning a high-performance bike opens up an exciting variety of other activities. Besides increasing your fitness, you can use your bike for vacation travel, for competition, to explore roadless areas, or to commute to work.

Since these activities can be enjoyed during the fine weather season for at least half the year, the big puzzle is why so few adults actually ride a bicycle regularly.

The Psychological Barriers to Adult Bicycling

The major barrier appears to be a series of beliefs based on experience with bicycles in the dim and distant past. These conditioned beliefs then serve as psychological blocks to taking up bicycling later in life.

As you have undoubtedly gathered if you have read this far, bicycles and bicycling are completely different from anything we may have experienced in years past. So changed are they that most of the negative beliefs that adults hold have become mere fantasies. For proof, let's examine some of the most common attitudinal blocks that seem to turn off adults from bicycling.

■ **BLOCK 1. Bicycling is too expensive. Why can't I ride a
cheaper department store bike? Besides, I already tried bicycling
and it hurt my knees.**

Not only is the typical $89.95 discount store special heavy and
cumbersome but if you live in hilly country, or must ride against
headwinds, its gears are usually inadequate to match the changing
terrain. The same is true of 3- and 5- speed bicycles. You find
yourself grinding the pedals as you struggle along in gears that are
far too high — a guaranteed way to stress the knees and other joints.
(A "high" gear is one where it is difficult to pedal uphill; a "low"
gear is one where it is easier to pedal uphill.) By contrast, joint
injuries rarely occur among bicyclists who ride a high-performance
machine that allows them to pedal briskly under all conditions.

**The secret of successful cycling — to make bicycling easy and
pleasant — a rider must spin the pedals briskly at a cadence of 60–90
r.p.m., or slightly more. It is this brisk pace that minimizes pressure
on ankles, knees, and hips and that makes joint injuries extremely
rare.**

By shifting smoothly from gear to gear, soaring up hills and then
down, an accomplished rider synchronizes the cadence of his or her
spinning pedals with the changing conditions of wind and terrain.
Whether riding uphill at 6 m.p.h., or downhill at 30 m.p.h., the
pedals continue to spin at approximately the same brisk pace while
the biker's entire body becomes a single fluid unit with the bike. To
glide almost effortlessly on silent wheels like this is what the joy and
fun of bicycling is all about. To many, it's the closest thing to flying
without leaving the ground.

Admittedly, riding like this does demand a minimal level of
fitness. But it isn't necessary to be a super-athlete. What is essential
is that you ride a modern, lightweight bicycle with a range of gears
wide enough to keep you pedaling briskly all the time.

Quality bicycles of this caliber can be found only in bicycle shops.
Bicycles sold in department stores and discount houses are invariably cheaper and heavier models with low-quality components intended for youngsters.

It has always amazed me that so many adults will unhesitatingly
part with thousands of dollars to buy a chromium-plated chariot
bristling with knobs and gadgets frankly designed to appeal to the
child in us all. Yet rather than lay out a few hundred dollars for a
grown-up's bicycle, all too many adults are satisfied to ride a children's model.

By riding a heavy, youngster's bicycle, you are locking yourself into casual bicycling—and probably ruining your knees in the bargain.

It's true that a quality bike costs several hundred dollars. Yet only on such a bike can you pedal briskly enough to maximize the health and fitness benefits of bicycling and to prevent joint injuries. Besides, you don't need a top-of-the-line model. A medium-quality road or mountain bike will get you into sports bicycling right away.

■ **BLOCK 2. I could never ride crouched over those turned-down, racing-style handlebars. I'd prefer to ride in an upright position, like on a 3-speed.**

A few years ago the choice in adult bicycles lay between a 3-speed and a 10-speed. Three-speeds are still available but their limitations lock you into the casual type of bicycling. Ten-speeds are also becoming hard to find. Most modern bikes have 12–24 speeds.

Most bicyclists prefer drop-style handlebars because they afford a variety of positions for your hands. By keeping your hands on top of the handlebars you can ride in a near-upright position. Few novices are aware, though, that on almost any bicycle drop-style handlebars can be replaced with a flat handlebar allowing you to ride upright at all times.

Better yet, you can ensure riding in the upright position on a top-quality bike by purchasing a mountain or all-terrain bike (ATB). Today the choice in adult bikes is between the lightweight road bike and the rugged 18–24 speed mountain bike or ATB (they're essentially the same).

Although you may have no immediate plans to ride up mountains, the mountain bike is beginning to emerge as the best thing that ever happened for the beginning mature rider. Not only is it a high-performance bicycle that can be ridden in the familiar upright position, but it comes equipped with a variety of climbing gears that will get you up most hills without having to walk. Its wide gear range will keep you pedaling briskly under all conditions. Its brakes are more efficient than those of a car. The saddle is more comfortable and can be raised or lowered at the flip of a lever. Risk of a puncture is less than with a road bike. And when used with lighter road tires, the mountain bike is a versatile machine that is equally at home on dirt roads, paved highways, or city streets.

If you want to race, there are mountain bike races. You can ride on dirt roads where traffic is minimal. And if later you decide to ride on rougher terrain, you have only to switch to fatter tires. Scores of veteran bikers are now recommending a mountain bike for the mature beginner.

"They're still relatively light and easy to pedal," says Frank Behrendt, president of International Bicycle Tours. "Many of our riders are over sixty yet they can keep going all day on a mountain bike. And if we meet any cobblestones or unpaved roads, those on mountain bikes have a much smoother ride."

■ **BLOCK 3. I can get the same health benefits riding a stationary bicycle.**

True! You can pedal indoors in any weather and achieve a high level of fitness. But riding the carpet can be excruciatingly boring and monotonous. Moreover, pedaling indoors in summer can become uncomfortably hot, and some exercise bikes are so noisy that you cannot hear music or TV.

Kenneth Cooper, M.D., exercise physician and author of *The Aerobics Program for Total Well-Being* (New York: Bantam, 1988), believes you are more likely to get a good workout when riding on the open road. His observations show that exercise heart rates are higher when riding outdoors. And stationary bicycling offers none of the joy and adventure of sports bicycling.

Incidentally, both road and mountain bikes can be mounted on a trainer and ridden indoors during winter.

■ **BLOCK 4. I could be killed by a speeding car. And what if I get a puncture or break a spoke or a control cable?**

Admittedly, bicycling is not completely without risk. The door of a parked car can be flung open in your face as you ride by. Or you can take a spill on gravel or on wet metal surfaces like bridges, rails, and manhole or sewer covers. However, most novices swiftly learn to avoid these hazards. Besides, most bicycle accidents not involving motor vehicles rarely lead to more than a few minor bruises, abrasions, or scratches. Even in the roughest off-road bicycle races, serious injuries are extremely rare.

If you stick to quiet roads and avoid highways filled with 18-wheelers and recreational vehicles, risk of being killed is statistically lower than while driving a car. Fewer than 1,000 bicyclists are killed in accidents involving motor vehicles each year, and half are children aged under 16. When you eliminate those riding at night, and those not wearing a helmet, fewer than 200 bicyclists aged 25 or over are killed in traffic accidents annually. This doesn't eliminate the need for careful riding. But it does emphasize that the risk of being killed while bicycling is grossly exaggerated.

Nor, provided you have a medical checkup before taking up exercise, are you likely to die from the exertion of bicycling. Only a handful of runners or bikers have died while exercising, and most of those had congenital heart disease. For every adult who dies while exercising, 100,000 sedentary people die at their desks or in bed. The risk of not exercising is thousands of times greater than any risk involved through exerting yourself on a bicycle.

And yes, you may have to handle a flat twenty miles from home, or replace a broken cable or spoke. But these skills are easily learned. And you never have to patch a tube on the road. Nowadays, you simply replace a punctured tube with a spare and wait till you get back home before patching the puncture.

Incidentally, you may also get rained on or encounter a stiff headwind — adverse conditions readily overcome by carrying raingear or by shifting down into a lower gear. The occasional barking dog can be repelled with a whiff of spray from a can of Halt, the same dog deterrent used and endorsed by the U.S. Post Office. At times, also, the weather can be hot and humid or it can be windy and cold. All of which indicates that bicycling is for real people who are active and alive, who love the outdoors, and who thrive on the joy of physical exertion.

■ **BLOCK 5. I simply don't have the time or energy for bicycling.**

Most of us can create more leisure time by watching less TV and fewer spectator sports. Anyway, if you can walk 3 miles in an hour or less without feeling tired, this is usually proof that you have ample energy and stamina to become an entry-level sports bicyclist. As you gradually pedal farther and faster each time, your body will mobilize the energy you need to ride longer distances. Many beginning bicyclists are able to ride 50 miles after only two months of practice.

If you cannot yet walk 3 miles in an hour, you should build up your walking speed to this level before investing in a bicycle. Alternatively, you can pedal an exercise bicycle the equivalent of 15 miles in 90 minutes. Should you experience fatigue after walking or pedaling, or if you have not exercised for a long time, or if you are overweight or a smoker, or have any other condition or dysfunction that can affect your ability to walk or ride a bicycle, you should see your physician before starting to exercise.

■ **BLOCK 6. My interest is piqued. But won't my friends and neighbors think I'm kooky if they see a mature, grown-up person riding a bicycle and wearing funny cycling clothes?**

The plain fact is that sports bicycling has become an upscale activity for upscale people, so chances are slight that others will think you "kooky." According to Simmon's Market Research Bureau, the greatest concentration of adult bicyclists are college graduates who are in the professions, or in managerial positions, and who have household incomes averaging $60,000.

This doesn't mean that you have to be rich or possess a graduate degree to take up sports bicycling. Ride a presentable, high-performance bicycle and wear a helmet, and you'll be welcomed at any club or group ride. No one really cares how much you earn or what you do for a living. Few bicyclists belong to country clubs and the majority prefer tennis to golf. But the people you ride or tour with will very likely be representative of the educated middle and upper-middle socioeconomic classes.

Typical occupations of bicycle club and tour members are physicians and surgeons, dentists, nurses, and other health professionals and also include airline flight personnel, writers and publishers, professional people, blue-collar workers, businessmen, executives, engineers, scientists, college professors and teachers, lawyers, accountants, stockbrokers, college students, housewives, and retirees.

The majority of adult bicyclists live in metropolitan areas or in college or university towns, or in sophisticated, cosmopolitan communities. Regardless of age they tend to be flexible, independent, individualistic, innovative, high-energy, outdoor-loving, young-at-heart people with a strongly positive attitude and a nonconformist outlook. They enjoy mild adventure, they seek moderate challenges, and they don't mind taking an occasional minor risk.

Meanwhile, sports bicycling is becoming increasingly trendy and fashionable. In the more fitness-oriented parts of America, owning a quality bike has become more of a status symbol than owning an expensive car.

Regardless where you live, or who your friends and neighbors are, once you become a dedicated sports bicyclist you are adopting a fitness lifestyle that automatically makes you a member of the burgeoning fitness culture.

Unfortunately, the majority of Americans still live outside the health and fitness culture. Millions of people blatantly ignore every recommendation by major health advisory agencies to stop smoking, to eat a low-fat diet, and to exercise. Whether you wear cycling clothes or a jogging outfit or tennis whites, all forms of exercise are alien to those in the couch potato culture. Yet the health and fitness culture continues to expand. As the baby boomers reach the 35–55 year age bracket, bicycling is becoming enormously appealing as a fun way to promote fitness and radiant health.

Whether or not all this makes bicyclists different from the rest of us is debatable. But if they are a special breed, you can easily join them.

Incidentally, although a helmet is virtually essential, you don't need any special bicycling clothes to begin with. Later, you may choose to wear them because they are much more comfortable and practical.

■ **BLOCK 7. Where I live there are too many hills.**

Chapter 3 describes how to equip your bike with the most powerful hill-climbing gears in existence, and in Chapter 8 you learn how to pedal briskly and without struggling, up almost any hill.

When she first took up bicycling, Ruby Curtis, a Chicago grandmother, quickly learned these techniques from members of her bicycle club. Within weeks, she told me, she became such a proficient hill climber that she deliberately sought out the hilliest rides. For one thing, she discovered that hilly rides were always more scenic. So passionately fond of hill riding did Ruby become that at age 59 she bicycled up the grandaddy of all hills — Colorado's Mount Evans, its 14,267-foot summit accessible only by pedaling 16 miles up the world's highest paved road.

■ **BLOCK 8. I can't keep up with younger bicyclists. I'd have to ride alone.**

Most older bicyclists have some difficulty keeping up with riders half their age. This is particularly apparent on some bike club rides. A group of younger riders, all on super-light road racers, will streak away in racing pack formation, leaving you feeling as though you were standing still.

Yet with the right bike and some preparation, an older rider can duplicate every other achievement of younger riders.

I myself cannot stay with the fastest riders in our local bike club.

Instead I often leave 10–15 minutes ahead of the pack and we all reach the halfway stop or café at the same time. There's no denying the pleasure of sharing an iced tea and social conversation with fellow bicyclists. So if you possibly can — and especially if you're a lone woman — I recommend joining your nearest bicycle club. (It is usually inadvisable for women to ride alone on the open road.)

Although most clubs concentrate on short, fast-paced rides for busy people with little time, there are also easier paced rides for beginners and for members with mountain bikes. In any case most mature riders are soon able to ride longer distances than most club rides cover, albeit at a more relaxed pace. Thus most clubs appreciate your offering to lead longer but easier-paced rides. This way, you'd always have plenty of company.

Outside metropolitan areas, many organizations like the YM-YWCA organize bicycling groups. Or an ad in the local weekly might turn up other like-minded individuals. However, even if you do have to bicycle alone, there are compensations. You don't have to ride with someone weaker who could slow you down, nor do you have to push yourself to keep up with a faster rider.

Speed excepted, mature riders can often equal or surpass many of the feats of more youthful riders. Last summer, for example, when I rode to the 10,500-foot summit of Colorado's Vail Pass Bicycle Trail, more than half of the hundred-odd riders I met appeared to be well over 40.

And age is seldom a barrier to joining a tour.

The Only REAL *Barrier to Bicycling*

As we've seen, most of the previous objections are illusions that exist only in the minds of nonbicyclists. For a more realistic appraisal, try asking an experienced bicyclist what he or she considers the biggest drawback to bicycling. It won't be hills, headwinds, or dogs. Almost invariably, the reply will be, "Cars, trucks, and RVs."

As you might imagine, there isn't much fun in bicycling on a narrow highway with a continuous stream of cars, 18-wheelers, and Winnebagos roaring past your left elbow.

So before you even think about buying a quality bicycle, ask yourself: *"Where can I ride it safely?"*

As a rule bicycle trails, parks, and residential streets are not satisfactory places in which to pedal a lightweight bicycle at 60–90 r.p.m. or more. Most bike trails and parks are full of joggers, walkers, and slow bicyclists while residential streets have too many intersections and stop signs. A bicyclist needs to be out on the open road with ten or twenty miles of uninterrupted riding ahead.

Begin by contacting local bicycle shops and officials of any local bicycle clubs. These sources can name all safe roads that exist. You can then drive out and check them over for yourself. Another excellent source of good biking roads are the numerous guidebooks for cycling in different areas, for example, the "25 Bicycle Tours" series of Backcountry Publications and the "Short Bike Rides" series of the Globe Pequot Press — which between them cover much of the northeastern United States.

Reject any narrow highways or roads that carry more than minimal traffic, or roads where the traffic is fast and includes many trucks and RVs. It's been my experience that the Southeastern states have the worst roads for bicycling, especially Florida, Georgia, Alabama, Mississippi, and Louisiana. Virtually every highway in south Florida appears narrow and clogged with lethal traffic.

Outside the Deep South conditions improve. Broad highways with wide paved shoulders are fairly standard in Texas, where in the scenic Hill Country hundreds of miles of paved, low-traffic backroads provide some of the finest open road bicycling in the Sunbelt. Great bicycling can also be anticipated in much of Colorado, Utah, Arizona, and California and in most of the Northwest, the Northeast, and the rural Midwest. In these areas local bicyclists have usually mapped out hundreds of miles of lightly traveled roads that are safe and pleasant to bicycle.

Consider dirt roads as well as paved roads. Several hundred miles of low-traffic dirt roads may be available, even though safe paved roads are few. In this case you should consider buying only a mountain bike. Superb mountain bicycling exists throughout the Rocky Mountain states.

If necessary, be prepared to drive out with your bicycle in your car for ten or twelve miles to reach the start of a safe bicycle ride. Don't expect to be able to start every ride from your front door.

Wherever you live, however, you absolutely must confirm the existence of safe roads, paved or unpaved, before you invest in a quality bicycle.

If there are no safe roads, then you're out of luck. You may have to be satisfied riding on bicycle paths. If so, you can improve your fitness to some extent by riding a heavy bicycle with fat tires and pedaling in the lowest possible gear (a mountain bike is a possibility). But you will never equal the health benefits of riding a high-performance bicycle on the open road. With the possible exception just noted, it won't be worth buying a quality bike. Better to learn this now than to lay out several hundred dollars for a late-model bicycle, only to have it rust away in the garage later on.

Assuming that you can ride safely, then let's continue and learn how to buy a bicycle that can really move.

CHAPTER 2

The Bicycle Technology Revolution — Aggressive Angles and Avant Garde Designs

Which bicycle should you buy? Certainly you should not rush out and buy just any bicycle. Yet most beginners are bewildered by the hundreds of bike models and their state-of-the-art components. To avoid the confusion, you must first understand the basics. And the initial step is to learn the names of all the principal parts of a bicycle.

So study Figure 2.1 and familiarize yourself with bicycle terminology. Begin to talk about a saddle instead of a seat. After that, read on to the end of Chapter 5. Even though it may sound a bit technical, and you may not understand it all the first time, try and grasp as many terms as possible.

Then go to a bike shop and identify all the parts you know the names of. Squeeze some brake levers and watch the brakes snap into action. Have a salesperson place a bicycle on a stand and allow you to spin the pedals while you move both front and rear derailleur levers through their full ranges of gear positions. Study how the derailleurs work.

Then ask the salesperson to release the front brake and to flip the front wheel quick-release lever. In just a few seconds the front wheel can be released from the bike. Ask the salesperson to show you the dropout slots in which the front wheel axle rests. If the salesperson isn't busy, ask him or her to remove the rear wheel also. Study how the brakes are released and examine the rear-wheel dropouts. (Dropouts are the U-shaped slots into which the axles fit.) Take a good look at every part of the bicycle including the freewheel and cogs, chainrings, pedals, hubs, spokes, rims, and tires. (The freewheel is the cluster of toothed gears near the rear axle. Each individual toothed gear of the freewheel is called a cog. Chainrings, also called chainwheels, are the toothed gears near the pedals.)

Along the way you'll discover that bicyclists frequently talk about *sets* as in headsets, framesets, wheelsets, tubesets, brakesets, and cranksets. *Componentry* refers to all the components—like handlebars, crankset, brakes, stem, and seat post—that are added to the frame to make it a bicycle.

Adult bicycles fall into two broad classes: *road bicycles* (formerly called "10-speeds"); and *all-terrain* or *mountain bicycles*. Each class gives you a choice of three types:

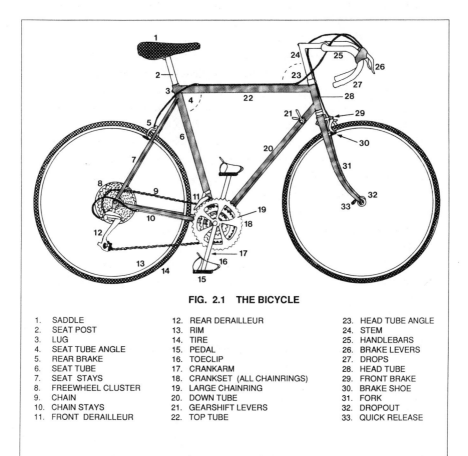

FIG. 2.1 THE BICYCLE

1. SADDLE	12. REAR DERAILLEUR	23. HEAD TUBE ANGLE
2. SEAT POST	13. RIM	24. STEM
3. LUG	14. TIRE	25. HANDLEBARS
4. SEAT TUBE ANGLE	15. PEDAL	26. BRAKE LEVERS
5. REAR BRAKE	16. TOECLIP	27. DROPS
6. SEAT TUBE	17. CRANKARM	28. HEAD TUBE
7. SEAT STAYS	18. CRANKSET (ALL CHAINRINGS)	29. FRONT BRAKE
8. FREEWHEEL CLUSTER	19. LARGE CHAINRING	30. BRAKE SHOE
9. CHAIN	20. DOWN TUBE	31. FORK
10. CHAIN STAYS	21. GEARSHIFT LEVERS	32. DROPOUT
11. FRONT DERAILLEUR	22. TOP TUBE	33. QUICK RELEASE

Road Bicycles	All-Terrain or Mountain Bicycles
Racing bicycle or road racer	Mountain racing bicycle
Sports bicycle	Mountain bicycle
Touring bicycle	City bicycle

Differences between these types are often quite subtle. Some makers have also produced hybrids such as a sports-touring model. However, each type of bicycle is designed and built to excel at a certain function. A road racer is built for speed while a touring bicycle is designed for extended long-distance travel while carrying a load.

To buy the right kind of bicycle you must first know what you will use the bike for. No single bike can do it all. You won't stand much chance of winning a road race if you ride a mountain bike, while a road racer is useless on a mountain trail. Thus you choose a bicycle for the type of riding you will do.

The snag is that most beginners don't know enough about bicycling to decide exactly what type of riding they want to do. Nor do they know how far they will go into bicycling. Most start out wanting to ride for fitness but few know whether they'll ever graduate to competition, whether they'll ride with a club, or take an extended tour, or become an off-road enthusiast, or ride to work. Most newcomers also hesitate to lay out several hundred dollars for a high-performance bicycle in which they may lose interest later on.

You can make a much better guess at the type of riding you will do if you know more about what bicycles are capable of doing, the components they are built of, and the types of bicycles best suited to adults.

Let's begin, then, by learning something about the frame and components that comprise a modern high-performance bicycle.

The Frame

Although a bicycle frame appears deceptively simple, the combination of design, geometry, and materials can make an enormous difference in performance, handling, and rider comfort.

On most medium-quality bicycles the frame consists of eight pieces of steel alloy tubing (called a *tubeset*) joined together by steel sleeves called *lugs*. Among the most popular alloys are chrome molybdenum (chromoly) and chrome magnesium. Most quality bicycles carry a decal identifying the type of alloy and the tube manufacturer's name, which is commonly Reynolds, Columbus, Champion, Vitus, or Tange. The decal may also indicate whether or not the tubes are butted. For example, it may say, "Guaranteed made with Reynolds 531 butted tubes, forks, and stays," or a decal on a mountain bike might be worded, "True temper chrome-moly triple butted."

Butting means that tubes are tapered thinner in the middle and thicker at the ends where they enter the lugs. Tubes can be double, triple, or quadruple butted, indicating increasing levels of thickness at the tube ends. For it is at the ends, where the tubes enter the lugs, that the greatest stress occurs.

Top-quality lugs, such as investment-case lugs, reinforce frame joints and minimize weakening of the tube caused by the heat of brazing (a type of soldering) during construction. Other top-quality lugs often have decorative designs that permit superior brazing at lower temperatures. These top-grade lugs distribute stress over a wider area at the joint than do cheaper lugs. To eliminate brazing altogether, many frames today are built of lugless tubing.

With or without lugs, almost all medium-priced bicycles have frames of dependably good quality. Using chromoly and other steel alloys, manufacturers are producing rigid frames that are uniformly strong and easily repaired. Butted frames are lighter and provide a livelier ride. With their smart new graphics and custom dualtone finish, these frames are often striking in appearance and design.

The Best Frame Materials

At present I recommend steel alloy as the best frame material for an entry-level bicycle. More expensive frames are available built of aluminum, titanium, and carbon fiber composites. But these have their minuses as well as their pluses. Frames of reinforced aluminum alloys are stronger than steel and dampen road shock well, but they can be costly to buy and expensive to repair. Nonetheless, aluminum frames — many with wide-diameter tubing — are becoming increasingly popular among advanced riders.

Titanium is also rigid, strong, light, and noncorrosive, but relatively few titanium frames are available and the majority are quite expensive.

For the frame of the future, carbon and other nonmetallic fibers bonded with epoxy appear to be the most likely replacement for steel. Their great stiffness, superior strength, light weight, good

shock absorption, and noncorrosive qualities make them an innovative new frame material. Within the life of this edition it is quite
conceivable that composite fiber may replace steel as the material of
choice for medium-quality frames.

Carbon and other fibers are used in one of two ways: they are
either made into tubes for conventional frame building; or they are
molded into a single frame unit. A single unit allows futuristic-
looking, aerodynamically designed frames that are smooth and
rounded to minimize wind resistance. Because it is particularly good
for damping road shock, polyethylene fiber is frequently used for
the rear wheel stays through which most vibration is transmitted.

The type of frame shown in Figure 2.1 consists of two triangles
and is called a *diamond* frame. Note the location of the head tube
and seat tube angles. Variations in these frame angles of only one or
two degrees can make a tremendous difference in comfort, efficiency, and responsiveness.

Changing frame angles requires corresponding adjustments in the
length of the chainstays. And the overall geometry is further bal-
anced by adjusting the rake, or curvature, of the fork blades. Thus
we have two extremes: slack and tight geometry.

Frames with Slack Geometry

These frames have a slack head-tube angle of 70–72° and an
equally shallow seat-tube angle of 72–74°. This makes for longer
chainstays and a greater fork rake. In turn, this creates a longer
wheelbase of 40–42¼″. (*Wheelbase* is the distance between the front
and rear axles.)

A frame with slack geometry means that it scores low on speed
and handling agility but that it offers superb riding comfort and
exceptional stability, especially when carrying a load at moderate
speeds. These qualities are prized for touring and mountain
bicycles.

Thus we find that mountain bicycles tend to have head angles of
70–71°, a seat angle of around 73°, and a wheelbase of 41–42½″ or
more. Touring bicycles typically have a head angle of 71–72°, a seat
angle of 71–74°, and a wheelbase of 40–42¼″. Many experts suggest
that a beginner buy a mountain bike with chainstays at least 17″ in
length and with a wheelbase of at least 42″.

Frames with Tight or Aggressive Geometry

These frames have a tight head-tube angle of 73–75° and a
correspondingly steep seat-tube angle of 73–76°. Such high angles

make for shorter chainstays, a steeper fork rake, and a short wheelbase.

This translates into superior control over a range of conditions important to racers such as delivering more power to the road, quick acceleration, fast cornering, stability at high speed, and nimble, responsive steering. These qualities are prized by racers, and the modern trend is to design racing bikes with increasingly steep geometry. Thus we find that the road racer typically has a wheelbase of 38–39½″.

Steeper frame angles are prized by racers because they result in a stiffer frame. The more rigid a frame, the less it flexes with each downstroke of the pedals. Thus less energy is wasted in flexing and more net energy is transmitted to the road. However, a very stiff frame can be uncomfortable for extended riding, which is why touring and mountain bicycles are designed with a more flexible frame and a longer wheelbase.

Midway between these extremes is the sports bicycle. Its head- and seat-tube angles typically range around 73° with a wheelbase of 39½–40″.

Frame Size Explained

At this point I should note that frames come in different sizes to fit riders of different heights. Frame size is calculated by measuring the distance between the center of the crankset spindle and the highest extremity of the seat tube.

Road bicycles come in stock sizes of 19″ (48 cm), 21″ (53 cm), 23″ (59 cm), 24½″ (63 cm), and 25½″ (65 cm). Some makers produce intervening sizes, while a few also make an oversized stock frame of 27″ (69 cm). Mountain bicycle frames are smaller and usually come in sizes of 16½″, 18″, 20″, 22″, and 24″, while women's mountain bikes customarily have 18″ or 19″ frames.

Forks, too, must be geometrically matched to the frame. Standard on all modern bicycles is the unicrown type fork, a crownless fork brazed directly to the steering tube. While the unicrown fork helps deaden road shock, mountain bicycles also have large-diameter fork blades and a clearly visible rake. Together, these features provide exceptional shock absorption. At present, most composite-fiber bicycles use metal forks.

A good indication of a quality frame is that in smaller frame sizes, as the length of the seat tube is reduced, the length of the top tube is reduced in proportion. This makes for slight variations in frame angles of smaller frame sizes.

You won't need to carry a protractor to measure frame angles. All specifications are quoted in the owner's manual and in the sales literature that accompanies each model. Thus to ascertain frame angles, or chainstay or wheelbase length, you need only consult the model's specifications. Comparison shopping for a bicycle is made much easier by purchasing a copy of *Bicycling* magazine's *Annual Buyer's Guide*, usually on sale for about $3 or available free when you subscribe to *Bicycling*. It gives full specifications on 300 different models.

Tip-offs to Quality

Other guides to frame quality are these. The overall weight of a typical racing bike is 19½–23 pounds, a sports bicycle 24–26 pounds, a touring bicycle 25–30 pounds, and a mountain bicycle 25–31 pounds. All other things being equal, the lower the weight the higher the quality.

Another indication of quality is that all better frames have thick forged dropouts brazed onto the frame. Vertical rather than angled rear dropouts are now preferred.

Touring and mountain bicycles should also be well supplied with components brazed on for all accessories. Both front and rear dropouts should have two sets of eyelets for attaching touring racks and mudguards. All these frames should have brazed-on cantilever brake bosses. (A *boss* is essentially a small, round piece of steel brazed onto the frame into which a bolt may be screwed.) If you buy a French-made frame, make sure it has English threads.

A quality bicycle will have all bearings sealed. Inexpensive bikes have nonsealed bearings, which means loose ball bearings are rotating against a tapered cone, a setup that requires frequent lubrication and periodic adjustment. By comparison, sealed bearings are shielded to keep lubrication in and dirt and water out. Bearings and ball races are contained in a single unit that can be replaced inexpensively when it wears out. You should certainly expect all major bearing sets to be sealed.

Also not recommended for beginners are folding or recumbent bikes. I say this in all awareness that the concept of a folding bicycle appeals to many. However, most folding bicycles cannot compare in performance with rigid-frame models, especially those with smaller wheels. However, if you are considering a folding bike, the Moulton series (small wheels) and the Montagu bikes (full-sized wheels) are worth investigating.

TOSRVPHOTO BY GREG SIPLE

The wide seat is one attraction of recumbent bicycles. However, many cyclists find them slow on hills.

One attraction of recumbent bicycles is that you can sit on a wide seat instead of a narrow saddle. But these bicycles seem slow on hills, and even veteran bicyclists have difficulty adjusting to them.

The Wheels

The lighter and more responsive your wheels, rims, and tires, the easier your bicycle will be to pedal and the faster it will go.

Bicycle wheels and tires come in three principal sizes, namely, in 26″ and 27″ diameters and in the 700 size, which has a diameter of about 26.7″. Wheels of 26″ diameter are used almost exclusively on mountain bicycles; 27″ wheels are used for sports and touring bikes; and 700 wheels, originally for racing bikes, are used nowadays also for most sports and some touring bikes.

Almost all tires in use today are clinchers, meaning they have a cross section like an automobile tire, and they are always used with an inner tube. Formerly most racers used tubular tires, a very light tire with a self-contained inner tube sewn up inside it. Today, however, clincher tires are available in such light weights that the advantage of tubular tires is rapidly fading. Tubulars are expensive, unsuited for touring, easily punctured, difficult to repair, and should be studiously avoided by the beginning adult. The best clincher tires have Kevlar beads and a belt of puncture-resistant Kevlar under the tread.

Inner tubes come in the same sizes as do tires. Two types of valves are used:

• *Presta,* or *needle* or *French,* valves are fairly standard on all better-quality road bikes. They are made of metal and will hold a higher pressure than Schrader valves. To inflate, unscrew the top of the valve and briefly depress it before inflating.

• *Schrader* valves are the same as those used on cars. They are fairly common on mountain bikes, although Presta valves are also available on 26″ tubes.

If you have any choice, always take Presta valves. Most tubes are of butyl and require inflating about once a week. Other tubes are made of polytex compounds. Bicycle tires should never be inflated at gas stations. Gas station pumps deliver large amounts of air designed to swiftly fill an automobile tire. Such a huge air flow can easily burst a diminutive bicycle tube.

Instead, you should carry a frame pump on your bicycle to fit the type of valve you are using. Be sure to buy the pump when you buy the bicycle and have the shop attach it onto the bike.

Pros and Cons of Rim and Tire Sizes

Rims of the 700 size became popular in America for two reasons: first, because they are the same size as rims traditionally used for racing with tubular tires; and second, because of the variety of tire widths available in the 700 size. These 700 tires are stocked by every bicycle shop today and are the most common size for racing and sports bicycles.

Nonetheless, 27″ wheels are still popular for touring bikes, and tubes and tires can be purchased in almost any small American or Canadian town. However, 27″ tires are seldom available in continental Europe, although they are found in Britain, Ireland, and New Zealand. Hence if you will do much touring in continental Europe, you may prefer to go with 700 wheels. 700 rims originated in Europe and tires are available all over that continent. Incidentally, 700 tubes, also available all over Europe, can be stretched to fit a 27″ rim.

Most 27″ and 700 rims will accept a choice of three or four different tire sizes. For instance, a 700 × 25 rim is compatible with these tire sizes: 700 × 20, 700 × 23, 700 × 25, and 700 × 28.

27 × 1″ tires, or 700 × 20, are the smallest and lightest, and also

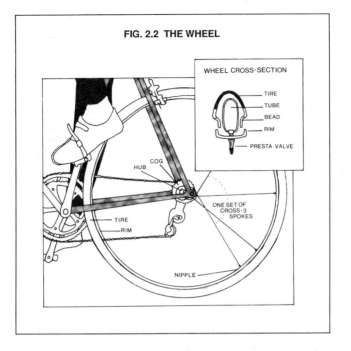

FIG. 2.2 THE WHEEL

the most easily punctured. They are for use on smooth roads for racing, training, and fast club rides. (There is also a 27 × ⅞".)

27 x 1⅛", or 700 × 25, tires are slightly larger and heavier and are for fast club rides and training on fairly smooth roads.

27 × 1¼", or 700 × 28, larger and heavier, are suitable for extended day rides and touring on all kinds of paved roads, including those with cattle guards. They can also be used for short distances on smooth unpaved roads.

27 × 1 ⅜", or 700 × 32, the largest and heaviest, are for touring with a heavy load, or for travel on fairly smooth unpaved roads.

Meanwhile, tires for mountain bikes range from the smaller 1½" road tire, good on both paved and unpaved roads, to the fat 1.95" or 2" knob-studded tire used for off-road travel on rough terrain. All mountain bike tires are compatible with the standard 26" rim. As a general rule, the larger and heavier the tire, the less the likelihood of getting a puncture.

With a little persuasion each of the 27" or 700 tire sizes can be mounted on most 27" or 700 rims, respectively. However, most rims are designed for a specific purpose and a specific tire. Hence a touring bicycle will have box-shaped touring clincher rims and they

will come in 3 varieties for use with 36, 40, or 48 spokes. Wheels
with 48 spokes are often used for tandems and for the rear wheels of
touring bikes designed to carry a heavy load. Generally, the more
spokes a wheel has, the greater the load it can carry.

Hubs and Spokes for Adult Riding

To minimize weight and air drag, racers prefer as few spokes as
possible and narrow, ultralight aero racing rims are available for
use with 28 or 32 spokes. In fact, modern wheel-building techniques
have now made the 32-spoke wheel fairly standard for both racing
and sports bicycles.

All other things being equal, for a racing or sports bicycle, I'd
always go for the lightest, narrowest rim designed to match the tire I
plan to use most. Modern anodized black or silver rims are among
the best available.

Most better quality bicycles today use a *freehub* on the rear
wheel. Freehubs employ what is known as a *cassette,* so called
because of its resemblance to a cassette tape player. Just as a cassette
tape slips onto and engages splines when it is placed on the spindles
of a cassette tape player, so a cog engages similar splines when it is
slipped onto the cassette of a freehub. (Splines are projections on a
shaft that fit into slots on a corresponding shaft, enabling both shafts
to rotate together.) But unlike a cassette player, which has room for
only a single tape, a freehub cassette has space for 6, 7, or 8 cogs,
depending on the model. In conjunction with a triple crankset, this
permits a bicycle to have as many as 24 speeds. For a more detailed
discussion see Chapter 3, "The Freewheel and Cogs."

Using the cassette system, the freehub permits quick and easy cog
changes while its superior axle support allows a stronger, longer-
lasting wheel.

Irrespective of whether or not a bike is equipped with freehubs,
almost all wheels today are built on low-flange hubs because low-
flange hubs offer superior flexibility and shock absorption.

Hubs and rims are laced together with spokes, using an asymmet-
rical pattern. The most popular pattern, known as a cross-3, means
that each spoke crosses 3 other spokes. A cross-3 lacing pattern
provides superior strength and durability while the wheel generally
remains true for a longer period. (A "true" wheel is without wobbles
and completely round.)

Butted spokes, which are thicker at the ends, are more flexible
and provide a more comfortable ride than do the slightly stronger

straight-gauge spokes. However, the best spokes are made of DT-stainless steel, a corrosive-resistant steel manufactured in Switzerland. Use of these spokes is a good indication of quality.

For a variety of reasons, some bicycles have wheels with different-sized spokes. When you purchase a bicycle, be sure to buy half a dozen spare spokes for each spoke size used on the machine.

Turn down any bicycle not equipped with quick-releases on both front and rear axles. Quick-releases allow you to remove either wheel at the flip of a lever. Any model without them is invariably a cheaper, less desirable machine. Quick-releases are invaluable when fitting your bike into a car trunk or shipping it in a box.

As with frames, the wheel of the future may be made of composite fiber. Such wheels, designed with just three or four fiber spokes, are already being used with success.

The Brakes

Today's brakes feel as if they are power-assisted. Their action is powerful and positive with almost no give. There are two types:
* *Side-pull caliper brakes* are standard on racing and sports bicycles, and on some touring models. They are operated by aerodesign brake levers in which the cable housing is concealed under the handlebar tape. This prevents use of shock-absorbing sponge grips on the handlebar top. If you prefer sponge grips, you must go back to looping the cables over the handlebar as in the days of yore. Center-pull caliper brakes are still seen on older models, and updated designs are now being reintroduced for use on mountain bikes. Older models are quite efficient and need not be spurned while the new models are considered at least equal to cantilever brakes.
* *Cantilever brakes* are standard on tandems, mountain bikes, and well-designed touring models. Powerful levers, often resembling those on motorcycles, actuate these center-pull brakes, which are mounted on bosses brazed to the rear stays and fork. These are excellent brakes that can swiftly stop a bike, even on a steep downgrade. If you plan to use both rear and front touring racks, check that these racks won't interfere with brake action.

While new brake types are appearing that use more sophisticated technology, most medium-cost road bikes are likely to have side-pull caliper brakes, while most mountain bikes and many touring bikes will continue to use cantilever brakes. Whether in dry or wet

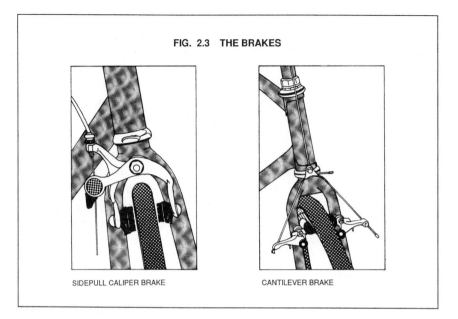

FIG. 2.3   THE BRAKES

SIDEPULL CALIPER BRAKE   CANTILEVER BRAKE

weather, or on any type of terrain, there seems little doubt that cantilever brakes have greater stopping power. Yet their larger size makes them inconvenient for racing and sports bicycles. Bearing this in mind, side-pull caliper brakes are considered more than adequate for the paved-road conditions on which racing and sports bicycles operate. Meanwhile, because of the extra loads they often carry, many touring bikes are equipped with cantilever brakes.

For medium-quality bikes, whether road or mountain, top brake brands include Diacompe and Shimano Dura Ace. For riders with small hands, special "short reach" or "junior" brake levers are available. Brakes of surprisingly good quality are available at very reasonable cost.

Check out brakes by squeezing the levers for signs of softness or sponginess, especially on the rear. Once the brake shoes meet the rim, good quality brakes have almost no give. You can learn how brakes feel by squeezing the levers on several different models in a bicycle shop. Reject any brake that feels spongy.

Stiff cables provide superior stopping power and are a good indication of quality. Cheap cables are flimsy and they stretch. Make sure that your brakes have a quick-release needed to open up the shoes when removing the wheel. Releases may be on levers, on cables, or on the brakes themselves.

Best avoided are auxiliary brake levers that parallel the top of the handlebar. Although they appear very accessible when your hands are resting on top of the handlebar, in practice these extension levers have so much "give" that much of their effectiveness is lost. Besides, they interfere with one's hand positions and add extra weight while most riders find they can reach the regular brake levers almost as quickly. Thus extension levers are usually found only on the cheapest bikes.

The Handlebars and Stem

Correct fit of handlebars and stem makes a big difference in riding comfort, especially for women.

Most riders prefer a drop-style handlebar for a road bike because it stretches the spine, takes part of the weight off the saddle, and permits a variety of hand positions. For example, you can place your hands on the drops, on the brake lever hoods, or on top of the bar. Crouching over with hands on the drops produces greater leg power and lower wind resistance, while riding with hands on top of the bar permits a near-upright position.

Handlebars come in three different widths and should be matched to frame size. The smallest, 38 cm wide, is for shorter men and women; the 40 cm width is for medium-tall men and taller women; while the widest, at 42 cm, is for people above average height. When purchasing a bicycle, it is usually possible to exchange handlebar or stem sizes without extra cost.

Correct Stem Size Can Streamline Your Look

The stem is for fine-tuning the rider's position. Stems come with extensions of varying lengths from 4 to 14 cm. The longest, 14 cm, is preferred by racers who like to crouch low and lean far forward. The shorter extensions allow you to ride in a near-upright position and to enjoy the scenery while touring. Shorter women should certainly opt for a short stem extension.

The stem also permits adjustment of the height and angle of the handlebars. On sports and touring bikes the top of the handlebar is usually positioned about one inch below the saddle height. Racers often prefer a lower setting. By raising the stem to its maximum height, however, you can attain a still more upright position. Not all stems are the same height. Some allow a higher position than others. If you adjust a stem to its maximum height be sure that at least two inches of the stem remains in the steering tube inside the head tube. Some stems have a minimum insertion mark above which they should not be raised. Otherwise, the stem could pull out or crack.

Various extension handlebars are now available permitting the rider to rest his or her arms on top of the handlebar while gripping a U- or triangular-shaped bar out in front. While these aerotype handlebars provide an undisputed aerodynamic advantage for experienced riders, they are primarily of interest to time-trial enthusiasts. I suggest passing them up until you gain more experience.

Mountain bikes use a flat handlebar with a sloping stem (see figure 4.7). The current trend is toward a narrower handlebar width than was formerly used. If you prefer, a similar type of flat handlebar can be fitted to most road bike models, thus allowing road bikes to be ridden in the upright position.

The Pedals and Toeclips

The toeclip-less pedal has revolutionized racing and is now available for sports and touring bikes. To enter a clipless pedal you simply engage the front of the cleat on the pedal and push down. To exit, you rotate the foot and the cleat releases like a ski binding. By locking the shoe directly to the bicycle, these step-in pedals maximize pedaling performance.

Cleats are small plastic or metal devices that are screwed to the sole of the shoe and that lock to the pedal. To function correctly, cleats for lock-in pedals must be very accurately fitted. If they are at all out of alignment, knee discomfort can occur. Moreover, clipless pedals are fairly expensive. Having cleats on the soles of your shoes can also affect your ability to walk. Some racing shoes have small, high cleats that make walking quite difficult. Cleats for sports or touring bicycles are often recessed or fitted in such a way that walking is easier.

Clipless pedals are *de rigeur* for racing and few racing bikes come without them. But sports and touring bikes are still available with pedals that accept toeclips and straps. Older rattrap pedals are also still made on which traditional toeclips can be fitted.

Improve Your Technique with Toeclips

For all road bikes not equipped with clipless pedals, I strongly recommend that beginners use toeclips and straps. Traditional toeclips come in four sizes: Small fits shoe sizes 4–8; Medium fits sizes

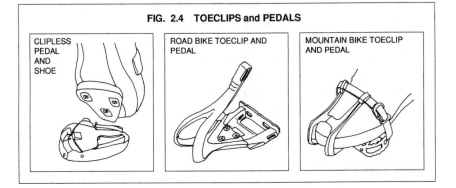

FIG. 2.4   TOECLIPS and PEDALS

| CLIPLESS PEDAL AND SHOE | ROAD BIKE TOECLIP AND PEDAL | MOUNTAIN BIKE TOECLIP AND PEDAL |

8½–10; Large fits sizes 10½–12; and Extra Large fits sizes 13–15. If you use a strap, place a twist in it under the pedal so that it cannot slide or move.

By a simple pull on the strap, toeclip straps can be tightened around the shoe as you begin to ride. They can be released in a jiffy by reaching down and placing the thumb on the buckle release. But since this takes some practice, I recommend not tightening the straps when riding until you gain some experience.

Tighten the straps only to the point where the shoe has a minimum of play but which still permits the shoe to be easily withdrawn from the strap. Many experienced touring riders never use cleats nor do they ever tighten their straps beyond this point. Even when quite tight, toeclip straps still permit sufficient play to prevent any knee misalignment.

Toeclips and straps are used to maximize pedaling performance by (1) keeping the foot in the correct position on the pedal; (2) holding the shoe as firmly to the pedal as possible; (3) allowing the rider to pull up on the pedal as well as to press down.

Mountain bike pedals have a large, wide beartrap shape that provides a nonslip gripping surface. A wide double carrier toe strap is available for mountain bike pedals in either medium or large sizes. Few riders tighten toeclip straps during off-road riding, hence the straps should be set to loosely hold the shoe in place. Without toeclips, your foot may slide forward off the pedal.

The Seat Post and Saddle

The combination of seat post and saddle can be finely adjusted to maximize rider comfort and efficiency.

The saddle is bolted to a clamp atop the seat post. In turn, this post (or pillar) fits snugly inside the upper part of the seat tube. Any desired saddle height can be obtained by sliding the post up or down in the seat tube. Once correctly positioned, the seat post is securely locked in place by tightening a bolt at the top of the seat tube.

The seat post is longer on mountain bikes — often 13″ or more — and it slides easily up and down inside the seat tube. It can be swiftly locked at any desired height by flipping a lever. This allows the saddle to be immediately lowered so that both feet are in contact with the ground for descending rough terrain.

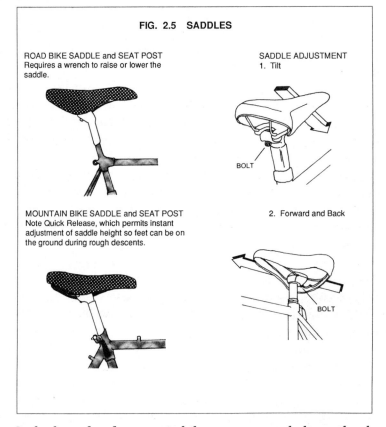

FIG. 2.5   SADDLES

ROAD BIKE SADDLE and SEAT POST
Requires a wrench to raise or lower the saddle.

SADDLE ADJUSTMENT
1. Tilt

BOLT

MOUNTAIN BIKE SADDLE and SEAT POST
Note Quick Release, which permits instant adjustment of saddle height so feet can be on the ground during rough descents.

2. Forward and Back

BOLT

On both road and mountain bikes one or more bolts on the clamp allow the saddle to slide toward the front or the back of the bike for a distance of about two inches. Simultaneously, it allows the angle of tilt of the saddle to be adjusted. These movements allow an enormous degree of flexibility in positioning the saddle for optimal comfort and pedaling efficiency.

At one time all saddles were made of hard leather. The famous English Brooks, or the French Ideale, saddles are still available and are prized by the elite. But it requires several hundred miles of riding to break in the conventional leather saddle and to mold it to your contours. To make this easier, new softened-leather types have been developed that can be broken in more quickly. Among the best is the original Brooks Professional saddle, readily identified by its large copper rivets. These saddles literally improve with age, both in comfort and appearance. With care they will last a lifetime. However, neatsfoot oil or another lubricant must be rubbed into leather saddles periodically while breaking them in and to keep them flexible later. These lubricants can easily stain light-colored shorts.

Nylon Saddles Can Still Be Elegant

Today most new riders opt for a nylon saddle with foam or gel padding. These saddles are less expensive and more comfortable than leather and require no breaking in. They come in all types, styles, sizes, and finishes including wider, softer saddles sculpted to fit the naturally wider female pelvis.

Many beginners believe that the large, wide-cushioned saddles used on children's bicycles offer greater comfort. This is usually erroneous because the wider the saddle, the more it chafes. Also, the soft cushioning compresses to zero under your weight, so that you're really sitting on the harsh metal shell underneath. In practice the most comfortable saddle is a fairly narrow man's or woman's touring-type saddle padded with form-fitting gel.

The gel-filled saddle is built on a shock-absorbing nylon base and is then covered with a soft, resilient pad of hydrostatic gel that flexes easily and distributes pressure evenly over a wide area. These and similar saddles are available in men's or women's racing, sports, touring, and mountain bike models. You can even get padded nylon saddles with a leather finish and copper rivets that resemble the finest leather saddles.

Actually the best way to prevent saddle soreness is to use a drop-style handlebar, thus transferring some of the weight from your rear end to your arms. Then by riding regularly and increasing the distance, you will develop muscles in your rear end that eventually overcome seat pain forever.

CHAPTER 3

*Go Higher, Farther, and Faster —
with These Hill-Gobbling Gears*

Most bicycle manufacturers seem to believe that their models are purchased exclusively by male athletes aged under 25 years. As part of this fantasy, stock bicycles are equipped with gears that are often much too high for the average mature man or woman. (The phrases "high gear" and "low gear" will be used repeatedly, so let me define them once again. A high gear is one where it is hard to pedal uphill, and a low gear is one where it is easier to pedal uphill.)

Despite having 18–24 speeds, touring and mountain bikes may still be geared too high to match the pedaling style of the average middle-aged rider. On road bikes the climbing gears are also frequently too high, and their range is too narrow, to permit many mature adults to maintain a pedaling cadence of 60–90 r.p.m.

At this writing, many bicycleshop salespeople are just beginning to understand the needs of bicyclists of both sexes who are more than 25 years old. They are learning not to deride gears lower and more powerful than those the manufacturer provides as "granny gears." And they are beginning to discover the varied options that are often available to enhance the performance of older riders. Frequently, a specific model can be ordered with a choice of crankarm lengths; with a choice of chainring sizes and shapes; and almost invariably with a choice of freewheel cogs. Each of these variables can have a dramatic effect on your bicycling performance.

If these options are not available, you can usually negotiate to have the desired changes made without extra charge when you purchase a new bike. Almost always the bike shop will make the required changes on the spot in order to close the sale, or the parts can be ordered and the changes made within a few days.

Even if you have an older bike, vast improvements in gearing can often be made very inexpensively by simply changing two or three cogs on the freewheel.

Gears

Never forget that the right bike is the one that lets you spin the pedals at a cadence of 60–90 r.p.m. or more. If you find pedaling uphill hard, the most likely explanation is that the bicycle you are riding has climbing gears that are too high.

Switching to a wider range of gears can do more to enhance your bicycling performance than any other single step. To maximize your performance — to conquer hills and headwinds — your bicycle must have a gear range wide enough to permit you to adjust your pace smoothly and accurately to a wide variety of conditions and terrain.

All too many adults are riding with an inadequate range of gears because they didn't know what to ask for when they bought their bikes. They just accepted the gears the bike came with. And many bikes sold to people in their 40s have gears that are better suited to a 20-year-old.

Bicycle Gears Made Simple

Understanding bicycle gears becomes much simpler when you understand the meaning of two terms: *speed* and *development.*

• *Speed.* This term, as employed in the phrase "14-speed bicycle," is used in the same way as in "a car with a 4-speed transmission." In the car you can place the gearshift lever in 4 different forward speed positions. Likewise, on a 14-speed bicycle you can place the gear-shift levers into 14 different positions or "speeds."

However, the actual gearing you get in each "speed" position depends on the sizes of the chainrings and cogs with which the bicycle is equipped. A 14-speed racing bicycle can have a very narrow range of gears while a 14-speed touring bike will have a much wider range of gears. Yet both bikes have the same number of speeds.

Taking it a step further, in some cases a 24-speed bike can have a narrower range of gears than a 10-speed — all depending on the number of teeth in the chainrings and cogs with which the bike is equipped.

- *Development.* The development of any chainring-cog combination is a number that tells you how high or how low that gear is. (As you will recall, a high gear is one in which it is difficult to pedal uphill while a low gear is one in which it is easy to pedal uphill.)

For example, a gear combination with a development of 21″ (a low gear) allows you to pedal uphill with much greater ease than does a gear combination with a development of 90″ (a high gear).

In everyday conversation, many bicyclists use the word gear rather than development. They'll say, "I was riding in my thirty inch gear." But what they really mean is a 30″ development.

It's essential to master the concept of development at this stage, because understanding development numbers is the only way to tell how low or how high any particular gear combination is.

Ask the average bicyclist what gear he is in and he'll probably reply, "I'm in my forty-two, twenty-one," indicating that the rider is using a 42T chainring and a 21T cog. This usage is fairly common among racers because almost all racing bikes have fairly standard 52T–42T chainrings and cogs in the 13T–23T range. Thus most racers will have some idea of whether this is a big, small, or medium gear.

But when someone says, "I was riding in my thirty-eight, nineteen," to be perfectly frank it doesn't signify much more to me than it probably does to you. Is this combination higher or lower than being in a twenty-four, thirty-two? Or is it higher or lower than, say, a forty-six, thirteen? Which of these 3 combinations has the greatest hill-climbing power? Or which would be best for a long downhill run?

For an accurate answer, you must know the development of each of these combinations.

What, then, is development? Any combination of chainring and cog sizes creates a development that is measured in inches. To calculate the development of any chainring-cog combination, you simply multiply the gear ratio by the diameter of the rear wheel in inches. The gear ratio is obtained by dividing the number of teeth on the chainring by the number of teeth on the rear cog.

Let's say you're using a 42-tooth (42T) chainring and a 21T cog (42 divided by 21 equals 2). That's a ratio of 2:1 or two-to-one. Your rear wheel is 27″ in diameter. When we multiply 27 by 2 we get 54″, which is the development of this particular combination.

In practice, you don't have to do any calculating to figure out the development of any gear combination. Table 3.1A provides gear developments for 27″ wheels and Table 3.1B does the same for 26″ wheels. For 700 wheels, use the 27″ table.

Assuming you have a 38T chainring and a 19T cog, entering Table 3.1A with these coordinates shows the development as 54″ (38 divided by 19 multiplied by 27 equals 54).

Why do these two different combinations have the same development, you may wonder? How can a 42T × 21T combination, and a 38T × 19T combination, both have a development of 54″?

Interestingly, at least half a dozen other common gear combinations all have the same 54″ development when used with a 27″ wheel. (Examples: 36T × 18T; 40T × 20T; 44T × 22T; 46T × 23T; 48T × 24T; and 52T × 26T.) And the reason, of course, is that they all have a ratio of two to one.

But when one rider says, "I'm in my forty-eight, twenty-four," while another says, "I'm in my thirty-six, eighteen," you'd never know that both are riding in the same gear. Whereas if each identified his chainring-cog combination by its development, they would both say, "I'm in my fifty-four inch development."

It doesn't matter what combination is being used to provide a 54″ development. When someone mentions a 54″ development, you immediately know it's the gear most adults choose when riding on the level against a light breeze.

An experienced bicycle tourist in his or her mid-forties will use the following developments when riding in each of the conditions named:

- 21″: climbing very steep grades
- 25″: climbing steep or long hills
- 35″: cycling up easier slopes
- 45″: cycling on the level against a headwind
- 55″: cycling on the level against a light breeze
- 65″: cycling on the level
- 75″: cycling on the level with a breeze at one's back
- 85″: cycling on a moderate downgrade or with a wind at one's back
- 95″: cycling downhill or with a strong wind at one's back

More About Development

The concept of gear development dates from the days of the high-wheeler. Because its high front wheel revolves once for every one revolution of the pedals, a high wheeler has a fixed ratio of 1:1. Hence if its front wheel is 54″ in diameter, it has a development of

Table 3.1A **Gear Development for 27″ Wheels**

Number Teeth Rear Cog	Number of Teeth in Chainring																	
	26	28	32	34	36	38	40	42	44	45	46	47	48	49	50	52	53	54
13	54.0	58.2	66.5	70.6	74.8	78.9	83.1	87.2	91.4	93.5	95.5	97.6	99.7	101.8	103.8	108.0	110.1	112.2
14	50.1	54.0	61.7	65.6	69.4	73.3	77.1	81.0	84.9	86.8	88.7	90.6	92.6	94.6	96.4	100.3	102.2	104.1
15	46.8	50.4	57.6	61.2	64.8	68.4	72.0	75.6	79.2	81.0	82.8	84.6	86.4	88.2	90.0	93.6	95.4	97.2
16	43.9	47.3	54.0	57.4	60.8	64.1	67.5	70.9	74.3	75.9	77.6	79.3	81.0	82.7	84.4	87.8	89.4	91.1
17	41.3	44.5	50.8	54.0	57.2	60.4	63.5	66.7	69.9	71.5	73.1	74.6	76.2	77.8	79.4	82.6	84.2	85.8
18	39.0	42.0	48.0	51.0	54.0	57.0	60.0	63.0	66.0	67.5	69.0	70.5	72.0	73.5	75.0	78.0	79.5	81.0
19	36.9	39.8	45.5	48.3	51.2	54.0	56.8	59.7	62.5	63.9	65.4	66.8	68.2	69.6	71.1	73.9	75.3	76.7
20	35.1	37.8	43.2	45.9	48.6	51.3	54.0	56.7	59.4	60.8	62.1	63.5	64.8	66.2	67.5	70.2	71.6	72.9
21	33.4	36.0	41.1	43.7	46.3	48.9	51.4	54.0	56.6	57.9	59.1	60.4	61.7	63.0	64.3	66.9	68.1	69.4
22	31.9	34.4	39.3	41.7	44.2	46.6	49.1	51.5	54.0	55.2	56.5	57.7	58.9	60.1	61.4	63.8	65.0	66.3
23	30.5	32.9	37.6	39.9	42.3	44.6	47.0	49.3	51.6	52.8	54.0	55.2	56.3	57.5	58.7	61.0	62.2	63.4
24	29.2	31.5	36.0	38.2	40.5	42.7	45.0	47.3	49.5	50.6	51.7	52.9	54.0	55.1	56.2	58.5	59.6	60.8
25	28.1	30.2	34.6	36.7	38.9	41.0	43.2	45.4	47.5	48.6	49.7	50.8	51.8	52.9	54.0	56.2	57.2	58.3
26	27.0	29.1	33.2	35.3	37.4	39.5	41.5	43.6	45.7	46.7	47.8	48.8	49.8	50.9	51.9	54.0	55.0	56.1
28	25.1	27.0	30.9	32.8	34.7	36.6	38.6	40.5	42.4	43.4	44.4	45.3	46.3	47.3	48.2	50.1	51.1	52.1
30	23.4	25.2	28.8	30.6	32.4	34.2	36.0	37.8	39.6	40.5	41.4	42.3	43.2	44.1	45.0	46.8	47.7	48.6
32	22.0	23.6	27.0	28.7	30.4	32.1	33.8	35.4	37.1	38.0	38.8	39.7	40.5	41.3	42.2	43.9	44.7	45.6
34	20.6	22.2	25.4	27.0	28.6	30.2	31.8	33.4	34.9	35.7	36.5	37.3	38.1	38.9	39.7	41.3	42.1	42.9

Developments not shown above may be calculated thus:

$$\textit{Development} = \frac{\textit{Number of teeth in chainring}}{\textit{Number of teeth in cog}} \times \textit{Diameter of rear wheel in inches}$$

Table 3.1B **Gear Development for 26″ Wheels**   43

Number Teeth Rear Cog	26	28	32	34	36	38	40	42	44	45	46	47	48	49	50	52	53	54
13	52.0	56.0	64.0	68.0	72.0	76.0	80.0	84.0	88.0	90.0	92.0	94.0	96.0	98.0	100.0	104.0	106.0	108.0
14	48.3	52.0	59.4	63.1	66.9	70.6	74.3	78.0	81.7	83.6	85.4	87.3	89.1	91.0	92.9	96.6	98.4	100.3
15	45.1	48.5	55.5	58.9	62.4	65.9	69.3	72.8	76.3	78.0	79.7	81.5	83.2	84.9	86.7	90.1	91.9	93.6
16	42.3	45.5	52.0	55.3	58.5	61.8	65.0	68.3	71.5	73.1	74.8	76.4	78.0	79.6	81.3	84.5	86.1	87.8
17	39.8	42.8	48.9	52.0	55.1	58.1	61.2	64.2	67.3	68.8	70.4	71.9	73.4	74.9	76.5	79.5	81.1	82.6
18	37.6	40.4	46.2	49.1	52.0	54.9	57.8	60.7	63.6	65.0	66.4	67.9	69.3	70.8	72.2	75.1	76.6	78.0
19	35.6	38.3	43.8	46.5	49.3	52.0	54.7	57.5	60.2	61.6	62.9	64.3	65.7	67.1	68.4	71.2	72.5	73.9
20	33.8	36.4	41.6	44.2	46.8	49.4	52.0	54.6	57.2	58.5	59.8	61.1	62.4	63.7	65.0	67.6	68.9	70.2
21	32.2	34.7	39.6	42.1	44.6	47.0	49.5	52.0	54.5	55.7	57.0	58.2	59.4	60.7	61.9	64.4	65.6	66.9
22	30.7	33.1	37.8	40.2	42.5	44.9	47.3	49.6	52.0	53.2	54.4	55.5	56.7	57.9	59.1	61.5	62.6	63.8
23	29.4	31.7	36.2	38.4	40.7	43.0	45.2	47.5	49.7	50.9	52.0	53.1	54.3	55.4	56.5	58.8	59.9	61.0
24	28.2	30.3	34.7	36.8	39.0	41.2	43.3	45.5	47.7	48.8	49.8	50.9	52.0	53.1	54.2	56.3	57.4	58.5
25	27.0	29.1	33.3	35.4	37.4	39.5	41.6	43.7	45.8	46.8	47.8	48.9	49.9	51.0	52.0	54.1	55.1	56.2
26	26.0	28.0	32.0	34.0	36.0	38.0	40.0	42.0	44.0	45.0	46.0	47.0	48.0	49.0	50.0	52.0	53.0	54.0
28	24.1	26.0	29.7	31.6	33.4	35.3	37.1	39.0	40.9	41.8	42.7	43.6	44.6	45.5	46.4	48.3	49.2	50.1
30	22.5	24.3	27.7	29.5	31.2	32.9	34.7	36.4	38.1	39.0	39.9	40.7	41.6	42.5	43.3	45.1	45.9	46.8
32	21.1	22.8	26.0	27.6	29.3	30.9	32.5	34.1	35.8	36.6	37.4	38.2	39.0	39.8	40.6	42.3	43.1	43.9
34	19.9	21.4	24.5	26.0	27.5	29.1	30.6	32.1	33.6	34.4	35.2	35.9	36.7	37.5	38.2	39.8	40.5	41.3

Number of Teeth in Chainring

Developments not shown above may be calculated thus:

$$Development = \frac{Number\ of\ teeth\ in\ chainring}{Number\ of\ teeth\ in\ cog} \times Diameter\ of\ rear\ wheel\ in\ inches$$

54″. And the pressure you place on the pedals to make one revolution on the high wheeler is exactly the same as that required for one revolution of the pedals on a modern bicycle using a 54″ development.

To make it clearer, the work and effort required to pedal a bicycle in a 54″ development is exactly the same whether you're riding a 52T × 26T combination, or a 36T × 18T, or a high wheeler with a wheel 54″ in diameter.

The reason why some bicyclists keep referring to meaningless combinations is that they are unaware that gear combinations are compared by their development in inches.

There are other benefits to describing your gear combination in inches of development. It helps you to understand why it takes exactly half as much work and effort per revolution of the pedals to climb a hill in a 22″ development as it does to climb it in a 44″ development.

You can understand development more easily when you consider it as analogous to walking a mile with big versus little steps. Biking in a high development (or a high gear) is like walking a mile with big steps—it takes a lot of effort. Biking in a low development (or low gear) is like walking the same mile taking little steps—it takes less effort and is much easier, although it will probably take longer.

When a development is multiplied by pi (3.141), the result is the distance that the bicycle moves forward at each revolution of the cranks. In a 54″ development, a road bike covers a distance of 170″. By comparison, using a 27″ development, the bike would cover only 85″.

Assuming it requires 50 foot-pounds of work to rotate the cranks one revolution in the 54″ development, disregarding friction, it would take 25 foot-pounds to rotate the cranks once in the 27″ development.

In either development, 50 foot-pounds must be expended to cover 170 inches. But in the 27″ development, you would exert only half the pressure on the pedals, making pedaling much easier, while stress on the knee is only half that when riding in the bigger 54″ development.

You Need Never Walk Up a Hill Again

Call that 27″ development a "granny" gear if you like. But if you use it, your knees may be in much better shape by the time you're a grandparent than if you strain up hills in the big 54″ development.

Although cycling is a nonimpact sport, riding uphill in a high development like 54″ (or even 44″) can exacerbate chondromalacia, or wearing away of the cartilage on the underside of the kneecap (see Chapter 10). Yet the lowest gear development on many racing bikes is 47″. That's partly because racers stand up on the pedals to climb hills. Yet standing up on the pedals is too strenuous for most mature adults to maintain for very long.

Most of us sit down to ride up hills. And even a 44″ development is too high for climbing most hills when seated in the saddle.

The Best Gears of Your Life

Hark back a moment to the list of developments and the conditions each is used for. They ranged from a low of 21″ to a high of 95″.

As you can see from the list, the 21″ or 25″ developments are much more suitable for climbing long, steep hills than are developments in the forties.

And unless you're hell-bent on speed, a high gear of 95″ is more than adequate for most mature adults. At the lower end of the gear range, you'll find that most mature and experienced bicycle tourists will have a low gear of 25″. Others go as low as 21″ or even 19″.

Though they may not often use these powerful hill-climbing gears, mature riders very wisely recognize that it is far better to have a couple of ultra-low gears they seldom need than not to have a really low gear when they need it.

Again, if you're able to jump on a road bike and take off up a mountain road, your personal gearing needs will be different. But if you're like most mature adults—fit and active but not a super-athlete—you can still bicycle up that same mountain if you use a lower gear development. You will pedal more revolutions. It may take a little longer, and your speed will be slower. But you will indeed get up that mountain road without walking.

In fact, you can bicycle up almost any hill—even hills in Colorado that are 40 miles in length—provided you have a range of gear developments that permits you to choose a pedaling rhythm you can stay with. For many older adults as well as many younger riders, that translates into a low climbing gear development in the 21-31″ range—and with a strong preference for the 21″ end.

Now let's take a look at other components that make up the drive train.

The Drive Train

Derailleurs and Shifting Levers

A pair of levers called *shifters* or *gearshift levers* operate the
derailleurs. The left lever operates the front derailleur, placing the
chain on one of the bicycle's two or three chainrings. The right lever
moves the rear derailleur, placing the chain on one of the five to
eight freewheel cogs. To make this happen you must continue
pedaling throughout a gearshift. In choosing which gear lever to
use, change the chainring (left lever) first and then make finer
adjustments with the right lever to the cog (see Chapter 7, "Master-
ing the Basics").

Since it's considered sportier to have the shifters on the downtube, that's where you'll find them on most racing and sports bikes.
On all-terrain bikes each lever is mounted separately, one on each
side of the handlebar, and you can shift gears at the flick of a
thumb. In fact, you can change both front and rear derailleurs
simultaneously.

Shifters are also sometimes placed on the stem, or at the tips of
the handlebars, or they may be actuated by handlebar twist grips.
Most experienced riders prefer the downtube or handlebar positions. On road bikes each lever has to be moved separately, one at a
time.

Until fairly recently all gear shifting was based on friction. To
shift gear you moved the lever to direct the derailleur onto the cog or
chainring you wanted. Then you adjusted it manually to run quietly
and smoothly. The lever remained held in that position by friction.
Each lever had a screw for adjusting its friction.

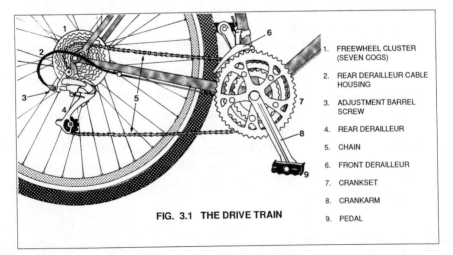

1. FREEWHEEL CLUSTER
   (SEVEN COGS)

2. REAR DERAILLEUR CABLE
   HOUSING

3. ADJUSTMENT BARREL
   SCREW

4. REAR DERAILLEUR

5. CHAIN

6. FRONT DERAILLEUR

7. CRANKSET

8. CRANKARM

9. PEDAL

FIG. 3.1 THE DRIVE TRAIN

Nowadays the uncertainty of shifting the rear derailleur has been eliminated by indexed shifting. Indexed shifters let you click into exactly the right preset position. By simply listening for the click that accompanies each shift, you automatically find the exact cog position. Many beginners liken it to tuning a push-button car radio. Thus indexed shifting has become standard on the rear derailleur of most modern bikes.

Indexed click shifters have obvious advantages, especially for racing or off-road riding where fast and accurate shifting is required. Yet they were mainly developed for beginners, and many experienced riders prefer to stay with friction shifting.

One reason is that gear settings are quite crucial. As cables stretch and cogs wear, indexed shifting may need adjustment. All it takes, usually, is a turn or two on a barrel screw. But not every rider has the mechanical aptitude to do this.

Nonetheless, given the choice between click or friction shifting, I'd always opt for indexed shifting.

The Crankset

Most medium-quality bicycles have Japanese cranksets (see Figure 2.1). (A *crankset* consists of two or three toothed gears near the pedals, called chainrings or chainwheels, along with the axle between the pedals, and the crank arms connecting the pedals to the axle.) Racing and sports bicycles usually have standard double 42T–52T or 42T–53T chainrings while touring and all-terrain bikes have triple cranksets. (A *double crankset* has two chainrings; a *triple crankset* has three.) A typical touring bike crankset will have 26T–44T–50T chainrings or possibly 26T–42T–46T. Standard on mountain bikes are chainrings with 28T–38T–48T or, preferably, 26T–36T–46T.

Since most bike shops carry small 24T and 26T chainrings in stock, these chainring sets can be easily changed to 26T–38T–48T or 24T–36T–46T, or any other desired combination. Usually this can be done without extra charge at the time of purchase. In other words, you usually don't have to accept the exact chainrings with which your bicycle is equipped at the factory.

If you plan to climb very steep grades on a mountain bike, you should investigate the Mountain Tamer Quad. It consists of an ultra-small chainring of 15T–19T that bolts on the inside of a triple crankset. This fourth chainring is normally used only on mountain bikes and is currently becoming available at mountain biking centers in Colorado and elsewhere.

Elliptical Chainrings

Chainrings can be either round or elliptical. Out-of-round chainrings have an elliptical computer-designed shape that perfectly matches the dynamics of leg movement for improved efficiency and pedaling power. The ellipse is very slight and difficult to detect with the naked eye. Currently one of the best elliptical cranksets is the Deore II Biopace HP made by Shimano. Nowadays, however, just about all Japanese cranksets are rigid, lightweight, and super-strong.

My experience with elliptical chainrings suggests that, during part of the pedal revolution, they provide the equivalent of being in a gear one step lower than the gear you are actually in. Thus they are clearly more effective, especially on hills. Since there is almost no price difference between round and elliptical chainrings, I strongly recommend an out-of-round (elliptical) crankset. The only drawback is that the smallest elliptical chainring has 26T versus 24T for cranksets with round chainrings.

Both round and elliptical cranksets offer a choice of crankarm length. Most brands come in the shorter 170 mm length and the longer 175 mm length. Some makers also supply very short 165 mm crankarms, an intermediate 172.5 mm length, and a long 180 mm length. However, these uncommon lengths are not always available.

Longer Crankarms

Naturally, the longer 175 mm crankarm provides greater leverage and more power when climbing hills. Depending on the gearing, using the 175 mm length can be equivalent to being in a gear one step lower than would be the case if using the 170 mm length.

Since most models can be ordered with crankarms of either length, I'd normally opt for the 175 mm crankarms if you are at least 5'6" in height and your bicycle's bottom bracket is sufficiently high to provide adequate clearance when cornering. (The *bottom bracket* is the short round tube holding the axle between the pedals, and to which both the seat tube and the down tube are attached.) If you are taller and there is adequate clearance, I'd certainly consider using 180 mm crankarms provided they are available. Most mountain bikes have bottom bracket clearance sufficiently high to permit the use of longer crankarms.

In any case I'd also consult the bike shop owner, or an experienced salesperson, for his or her opinion. Shorter men, and especially shorter women, should probably stay with 170 mm or 172.5 mm crankarms. And very short people will probably prefer a 165 mm crankarm (usually available only for road bikes).

Together, longer crankarms plus elliptical chainrings can contribute appreciably to your hill-climbing ability. But longer crankarms are not advised for shorter people because they can distort hip movement, causing the rider to rock from side to side. I recommend that shorter people rely on gearing to improve hill-climbing power.

The Freewheel and Cogs

A freewheel contains the pawls that click around and allow you to coast without pedaling. However, the term *freewheel* usually includes the cluster of five to eight cogs mounted on the freewheel body (or cassette) that makes multigeared bicycling possible.

Freewheels come in two distinct types:

• *The conventional freewheel body* on which cogs are screw-threaded one by one to form a cluster. These cogs are spaced a standard 3.5 mm apart. The freewheel cluster is then screwed onto a thread on the rear wheel hub. To remove it, you require a special key or *freewheel remover.*

• *The freehub,* a more recent concept in which the actual freewheel is housed inside a plastic cassette attached to the wheel hub. The cassette contains splines, or projections, similar to those on the spindle of a cassette tape player. Like a cassette tape, each cog fits over the splines on the freewheel cassette. From five to seven cogs can be placed, one by one, onto the freewheel cassette. The eighth, or final, cog is threaded, and is screwed onto the tip of the cassette to lock the other cogs in place.

On a freehub the cogs are spaced only 2.7 mm apart and a special narrow chain must be used. These chains, incidentally, are narrow only on the outside. On the inside, they are standard-sized and will thus fit conventional cogs and chainrings.

While European freewheels are still available, most freewheel production today is Japanese. Among Japan's newest innovations is the Hyperglide concept, in which each cog has 4 sculpted steps that help the chain move over the freewheel. As a result, the Hyperglide system is currently the fastest and smoothest shifting system made. Furthermore, you can shift down without having to ease up on pedal pressure as you must do with all conventional shifting systems.

The Superglide concept is an even more recent Japanese invention. By using chainrings with uneven tooth profiles, Superglide permits the chain to glide smoothly from one chainring to another even while climbing a hill under full load. Both Hyperglide and Superglide are currently available on mountain bikes.

More Speeds Don't Mean Lower Gears

Having 24 speeds doesn't necessary mean that you will have climbing gears that are lower than those available on an 18-speed. Whether you have 6, 7, or 8 cogs, most racing bikes come with a freewheel range of 13T–24T, the standard sports bike has 13T–26T, while most touring and mountain bikes come equipped with 13T–28T or 14T–30T. Larger cogs must usually be custom-ordered. The more teeth on the largest cog, the lower the gears you will have.

Far from giving you lower climbing gears, the 7- or 8-cog freewheels simply provide more intermediate gears. Moreover, in some types, the largest cogs I could find had only 28T or 30T while the smallest had to be 12T or 13T because only these sizes had the locking thread.

I think the freehub concept is great provided that you can get cogs large enough to match the needs of mature riders. The large 32T cog I recommend for all mature bikers is available on at least one freehub system (the Deore XT) and by now may be available on others. But with some freehub systems you may be stuck with a virtually useless 12T or 13T cog at the high end of your gear cluster because only these small cogs may contain the locking thread.

To sum up: provided you can obtain the cog sizes recommended later, I'd go with a freehub system every time. The freehub systems are also compatible with both narrow-chain and indexed shifting systems. In fact, all are standard on most modern oriental bikes.

Make Your Own Gear Development Chart

If you've followed me so far, you already know more than many bicyclists who've been riding for years. In fact, you're already so far along that you can quickly learn to make a gear development chart for any bicycle — even a 24-speed. To many bicyclists, these are also known as *grid charts*.

All you need to know is this.

Almost all multigeared bicycles have either two chainrings (a double) or three chainrings (a triple). Meanwhile, freewheels may have from five to eight cogs. Multiply 3 chainrings by 8 cogs and you have 24 speeds, or 2 chainrings by 7 cogs for 14 speeds.

The number of teeth on a chainring is usually stamped on its side. If not, you can count the number of teeth on each chainring. And you can easily count the number of teeth on each cog by flipping the quick-release and removing the rear wheel.

Let's say you have a mountain bike with a triple crankset that has 26T–38T–48T chainrings and that has 6 cogs with 14T–16T–20T–22T–27T–32T. Using the 26″ wheel gear table given earlier in this chapter, you can easily make a development chart corresponding to Grid Chart 3.1.

Grid Chart 3.1: **Developments Compatible with Crossover Shifting for a Bicycle with Triple Crankset**

		Cogs					
		32	27	22	20	16	14
Chain Rings	48			46	57	62	78	89
	38		31	37	45	49	62	71
	26		21	25	31	34	42	

Many bikers carry a similar grid chart attached to their handlebars or handlebar bags. By glancing down at their drive train, they can immediately identify which development they are in and they can decide to which development they may wish to shift next.

Note that no developments are shown for the 48T × 32T and the 26T × 14T combinations. That's because, with a triple crankset, the chain angle in these speeds is so oblique that pedaling isn't practical. Thus our 18-speed bike really has only 16 working gear positions, and a 24-speed may have as few as 20 speeds that actually function. Even with a double crankset, you may have to sacrifice one speed when using the smaller chainring.

Avoid Gearing with Duplicate Positions

Something to watch for is the number of duplicate, or near-duplicate, gear positions. For example, our Grid Chart 3.1 has two positions with identical developments of 31″ and two others with duplicate 62" developments. Then there are two near-duplicates of 45" and 46". The difference between riding in a 45" or 46" development is so slight that it isn't worth shifting for.

At the lower end of the gear range, it's also hardly worth shifting for gears as closely spaced as 45" and 47", nor at the higher end for developments as close as 75" and 78". Such gears are called *near-duplicates*.

Thus on Grid Chart 3.1 we have two sets of duplicates and one set of near-duplicates. This eliminates three gear positions. While it isn't always possible to eliminate duplicates and near-duplicates entirely, the fewer you have in your gearing, the better.

Duplicates and near-duplicates often can be eliminated. You won't find a single one on Grid Chart 3.2 for a 15-speed touring bike:

Grid Chart 3.2:   **Developments Compatible with Alpine Shifting for a 15-Speed Road Bicycle**

				Cogs		
		30	26	21	17	14
Chain Rings	46		48	59	73	89
	42	38	44	54	67	81
	26	23	27	33	41	

Double Shifting

Two distinctly different gear shifting patterns can be used to shift through the gear sequence of any multigeared bicycle.

• *Alpine shifting* means shifting up or down one gear step at a time. In Grid Chart 3.1, for example, to shift step by step from the lowest to the highest gear means shifting from the 21" development to 25", 31", 34", 37", 42", 45", 49", 57", 62", 71", 78", and 89" — a total of 13 gear positions.

To do this requires at least six double shifts. That is, you must shift to a different chainring, and then shift up or down one or two cogs. To go from 34" to 37", for example, you must shift up to a larger chainring by moving the left lever, then you must move from the 20T cog to the 27T cog by moving the right lever.

Double shifting means you must shift both front and rear derailleurs to move up or down to the next gear position in the sequence. A shifting pattern like this, involving frequent double shifting, is known as alpine shifting.

Racers don't have time for such intricate maneuvering. They use a different shifting sequence known as crossover shifting.

• *Crossover shifting* involves making only a single double shift, or crossover, between each two chainrings. Crossover shifting accomplishes this by sacrificing one or more of the least useful gears.

Using Grid Chart 3.1 again, the crossover shifting pattern would go from 21″ to 25″, 31″, 34-D-37″, 45″, 49″, 62″, 71-D-78″, and 89″ (D signifies a double shift). Out of a total of 13 possible gear positions, only 10 are commonly used. But the result is an easily remembered shifting sequence for which grid charts are seldom needed.

Alpine versus Crossover Shifting

Although virtually any multiple-gearing system can be shifted using either the alpine or the crossover pattern, it is possible to design gearing that is much more compatible with one of these shifting patterns than with the other.

For example, the gearing in Grid Chart 3.1 is more compatible with crossover shifting while the gearing in Grid Chart 3.2 is better suited to alpine shifting. While it does take 4 double shifts to move through the entire Grid Chart 3.2 sequence, only the shift from 33″ to 38″ requires a complicated two-cog shift with the right lever. The three remaining double shifts are relatively simple.

These shifting patterns are as applicable to double chainring systems as they are to those with triple chainrings.

Moreover, freewheel clusters are often designed to facilitate one shifting pattern rather than another. The gearing on virtually all racing bikes, and on most sports bikes, is compatible with crossover shifting. Crossover freewheels have wider steps between the larger cogs and closer steps between the smaller cogs. This inevitably creates several duplicate or near-duplicate positions. Yet by sacrificing near-duplicates on the larger and smaller chainrings, crossover gearing permits you to stay in the middle chainring most of the time, using a double shift only when it becomes necessary to switch to the larger or smaller chainrings.

This causes all the gear positions to be bunched up at the high gear end—a situation that most racers seem to prefer.

Alpine Gearing Is Best for Touring

In alpine freewheels gears are more equidistantly spaced and near-duplicate positions are fewer. Because it allows a greater choice of intermediate gears, alpine gearing is preferred by most touring, and by many off-road, bicyclists. To shift through the entire sequence requires several double shifts. But these riders prefer double shifts to riding uphill in high gears. Besides, on a mountain bike with thumb shifters, double shifts are quick and easy to make.

Moreover, since you can shift through any gearing system in either an alpine or a crossover pattern, you don't have to go through every intervening gear when you shift. Using Grid Chart 3.1, a rider approaching a steep hill will typically shift direct from the 78″ position to the 34″ one by dropping down two chainrings and by shifting down one cog.

When considering any bike, you should make a gear chart for that bike and consider to which shifting pattern the gearing is most compatible. Then ask yourself if that is the shifting pattern you'll actually want to use. If not, you can usually change over by judiciously switching some of the cogs.

Design Your Own Gearing

Most experienced bicyclists design their own gearing systems. First they decide on the number of speeds and on the range of gear developments they will want. Then, using the appropriate gear table, they juggle chainring and cog sizes to approach as closely as possible to the developments they prefer. Usually this requires some minor tradeoffs. But if you've followed this book so far, you should have no difficulty designing your own gearing system.

Let's say, for example, that you have a touring bike with 27″ wheels and that you'd like an 18-speed system compatible with alpine shifting. The bike is already fitted with a triple crankset having 26T–44T–50T chainrings. The developments you want range from 22″ to 25″, 30″, 35″, 40″, 45″, 50″, 55″, 60″, 65″, 70″, 75″, 80″, 85″, and 95″.

First, prepare a grid chart thus:

		32	Cogs	14
Chain Rings	50			96
	44	37		85
	26	22		

Using the 27″ wheel gear table, it swiftly becomes apparent that to achieve a high gear of 95″ and a low gear of 22″, the outside cogs must be 14T and 32T, respectively. After that, it doesn't take much juggling to figure out that the remaining cogs must be 17T, 20T, 24T, and 28T. Despite at least two near-duplicates, the completed Grid Chart 3.3 comes very close to supplying all the developments you desire. Because you chose equidistantly spaced gears, your gearing system is most compatible with alpine shifting.

Grid Chart 3.3: **Developments Compatible with Alpine Shifting for an 18-Speed Bicycle**

		Cogs					
		32	28	24	20	17	14
Chain Rings	50		48	56	67	79	96
	44	37	42	49	59	70	85
	26	22	25	29	35	41	

Most desired gearing changes can be achieved inexpensively by simply changing cogs. If you fit large cogs where there were small cogs before, you may have to install a larger capacity derailleur also. Switching small chainrings is equally inexpensive. Other than that, it's invariably cheaper to make changes to your freewheel than to your crankset.

Which Gearing Is Best?

That depends on the individual rider, of course. But if I were to generalize, I'd suggest that the average beginning adult would do well to consider a triple crankset matched to a freewheel cluster to provide a range of gears with developments from 21″ or 22″ to around 90″.

Regardless whether you buy a racing or a sports bike, or a touring or a mountain bike, you can safely buy one that has a triple crankset. In response to the growing demand from mature riders, some makers are beginning to produce racing bikes with triple cranksets while triples are fairly common on sports bikes and triple cranksets are taken for granted on touring and mountain bikes. Having a triple crankset makes it much simpler to install the low climbing gears that most nonathletic adults need to pedal uphill.

On a sports bike, I'd aim for a 26T–44T–50T triple crankset and on a touring bike for a 26T–42T–46T chainring combination. For a mountain bike, chainrings with 24T–36T–46T would seem most ideal with 26T–38T–48T as second choice. Most stock mountain bikes have 26T–36T–46T or 28T–38T–48T chainring sets. In most cases, I recommend replacing the factory-installed small chainring with another that has fewer teeth.

For touring and mountain bikes, I'd also prefer an alpine shifting pattern.

Almost without exception then, I'd recommend a freewheel cluster with from 14T–32T. Most stock mountain bikes have 13T–28T cogs while road bike freewheels have an even narrower range. Some bike shops may have to custom-assemble a conventional freewheel with 14T–32T. However, I've generally found that conventional 14T–32T clusters are readily available, often quite inexpensively.

On this basis the gearing in charts 3.1, 3.2, and 3.3 should be eminently suitable for most beginning adult riders. To add to my recommendations, you might consider the crossover-compatible gearing system given in Grid Chart 3.4 for a mountain bike.

Grid Chart 3.4:   **Developments Compatible with Crossover Shifting for an 18-Speed Bicycle**

		Cogs					
		32	28	24	20	17	14
Chain Rings	48		46	54	65	76	93
	38	32	37	43	51	60	73
	26	22	25	29	35	41	

A Double Chainring System

You may have to hunt around but double cranksets can be found with chainrings in the 28T–42T range. In fact, one of the most experienced bicycle tourists I know uses the system illustrated by Grid Chart 3.5.

Using a crossover shifting pattern, he simply moves up from 24″ through 27″, 31″, 38″, 45″, 54-D-57″, and 67″ to 81″ — employing a total of 9 commonly used gears. Should he be going too fast for his 81″ top gear to keep pace, he coasts until his speed drops back

Grid Chart 3.5: **Developments Compatible with Crossover Shifting for a 12-Speed Bicycle**

		Cogs					
		32	28	24	20	17	14
Chain	42	35	40	47	57	67	81
Rings	28	24	27	31	38	45	54

down. His rationale is that if he's going too fast for his 81" development to keep pace, he'll be needing his brakes rather than a higher gear.

A double chainring system like this could supply virtually all the gears needed by the average mature adult, whether for touring, off-road riding, or even for day rides on a sports bike.

The Key to Success in Adult Bicycling

Never lose sight of this fact: Of all the variables that can enhance your bicycling performance, having the right gear development for each of your speeds is the most vitally important factor.

A good general guide is that most stock bikes have small chainrings that are too large and large cogs that are too small to match the capabilities of most mature riders.

When you match smaller chainrings with larger cogs — and add such boosters as elliptical chainrings and longer crankarms — you create tremendously powerful gear developments that can take you soaring up hills, or that can help you ride all day without becoming fatigued.

CHAPTER 4

How to Choose the Right Bicycle

Choosing the right bicycle saved Hartley Alley's life.

Hartley, a college professor, took up bicycling back in 1959. At that time he weighed 195 pounds and smoked two packs of cigarettes a day. An electrocardiogram showed that one of his coronary arteries was already completely occluded.

"I had to do something to get back into shape," Hartley told us. "Cycling seemed like a fun way to exercise."

Right off, Hartley bought a road racer with big gears and tried to keep up with a younger, fast-riding crowd. But the big gears tore up his knees and he had to quit bicycling for six full months.

Hartley used his enforced rest to learn more about bicycling. He soon realized that the reason his bike was stashed away in the garage was due more to lack of know-how than to lack of physical ability. With a more suitable bike, he was sure he could do better.

Hartley sold the road racer. And as soon as he could ride again, he bought a lightweight touring bike with a wide range of gears. In a short while he was riding every day. His wife Jean also took up bicycling and they began to take touring vacations together. Hartley noticed dramatic improvements in his performance when first he quit smoking and then, a few months later, he went on a low-fat diet that he has maintained ever since.

As later electrocardiograms showed his heart developing a new artery system, Hartley's physician credited bicycling for saving his life. His heart is now as good as new without surgery or drugs.

After finding the right bicycle, Hartley Alley at age 68 set out on a 2,238-mile tour from Colorado to Massachusetts.

"If I hadn't found the right bike, I'd be dead today," Hartley told me. "Once I learned what bike I needed, I went from a fat slob lighting one cigarette after another to a trim, athletic 150 pounds in a single year."

Since then, Hartley and Jean have bicycled together all over the world, including China. And for 14 years they operated the Touring Cyclist, a Boulder, Colorado firm that pioneered the concept of nylon touring bags.

To celebrate his retirement, at age 68 Hartley bicycled 2,238 miles from Boulder, Colorado to Lynn, Massachusetts to attend his fiftieth high school reunion. En route, Hartley carried a mobile ham radio transceiver and maintained constant radio contact with other ham operators as he pedaled along.

For this trip, Hartley knew he would need *exactly* the right bicycle. So he had a special touring model custom built by Lieper of

Boulder, Colorado. Weighing only 25 pounds, it has 21 speeds and a
gear range of 25"–106".

"That was exactly the right gearing for me," Hartley said. "When
I reached Lynn, I easily rode up the steep, fifteen percent grade to
my boyhood home. Which is something I could never do on the
bikes we had as a boy."

Hartley's experience bears out what I've been saying all along:
that choosing the right bike to begin with dramatically reduces any
chance that you will want to give up on bicycling later.

What you are seeking, of course, is a good match between bicycle
and rider. And that can be achieved only by considering your long-
term bicycling needs. Thus if you expect to become fitter than you
are at present, and able to ride farther and faster, you should get the
best entry-level bicycle that your money can buy. That still translates into a medium-quality bicycle. You don't need an Italian road
racer or a custom-built touring bike yet.

But you still need to know which type of riding you expect to do.
So to help you decide, let's take a look at each of the types of bicycles
you can choose from.

Road Bicycles

Weighing 22–27 pounds and equipped with skinny tires, road
bikes are designed to glide gracefully on paved roads with a minimum of effort. The majority have 10–24 speeds and drop-type
handlebars, and they are used for fitness training, day rides, racing,
and touring.

Road Racing Bicycles

Most people buy racing bicycles because of their sexy, sporty
look. They have no more intention of racing than does the average
sports car owner. But if you plan to ride competitively, or in
triathlons or Masters races — or if getting ahead of the pack in club
rides is your aim — then this is your bike. Its lightweight frame,
rims, and tires let you cover longer distances in less time, and no
additional skill is needed to ride it. But owning a road racer limits
you to a type of riding primarily built around fast, short rides.

A racing bike's aggressive frame geometry makes it a mediocre
choice for touring, and its poor shock absorption makes it uncomfortable for all-day rides. Its narrow, delicate tires are vulnerable to

punctures. Too, its high gears are designed for standing on the pedals as you "honk" up hills. Thus if you sit down to a climb, you can tear up your knees.

Although gears can be altered, most racers habitually use closely spaced gears. And these big gears need legs and lungs that most adult newcomers don't yet have.

If your goal is recreational riding — day rides and touring — a road racer can be an unwise choice. Its load-carrying capacity is poor and stock models lack the gears for easy climbing.

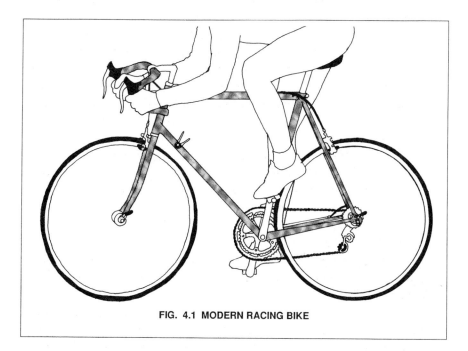

FIG. 4.1 MODERN RACING BIKE

If you do opt for a racing bike, you won't need an expensive model. Competition among manufacturers is so intense that virtually every medium-priced road racer features such advances as step-in pedals, tight frame geometry, and a geometrically matched fork. So little difference exists among most makes that they all tend to have steep-angled frames with short chainstays plus top Japanese drive trains and componentry. They have two chain rings and six, seven, or eight cogs. And most come equipped with 700-size wheels and lightweight clincher tires. (*Note:* newcomers should avoid any road racer equipped with tubular tires.)

Sports Bicycles

Sports bicycles are equipped with slightly less expensive componentry than racing bikes but have greater durability and a wider gear range, and they provide a more comfortable ride. Sports bikes usually have either 700 × 25 or 700 × 28 tires, or they may have 27" wheels with 1⅛" or 1¼" tires.

Most sports bikes have two chainrings and six, seven, or eight cogs, providing a total of 12, 14, or 16 speeds. You can quite easily convert a sports bicycle into a near-facsimile of a touring bicycle by installing a triple crankset, thus endowing it with 18 or more speeds. You should also switch to 700 × 28 tires or to 27" by 1¼".

Alternatively, you can upgrade a lightweight sports bicycle into an entry-level road racer (good for novice races only) by installing lighter-weight tires. If the sports frame has a slack seat angle, such as 72° rather than the 73–76° found on road racers, you can compensate by sliding the saddle as far back from the handlebars as it will go. This will give you riding power almost equal to that of a racing bike.

These modifications allow you to try racing or touring with a sports bicycle. With or without these changes, however, a sports bicycle is an excellent beginner's choice for fitness riding and for day rides.

Touring Bicycles

Touring bicycles, or road cruisers, are a compromise between the geometry of a sports bicycle and the low climbing gears found on mountain bikes.

However, to achieve maximum comfort, chainstays are made longer while both head and seat angles are often as slack as 71.5°. Add on more fork rake to lengthen the wheelbase to 40–42¼", and you have a superbly comfortable bicycle that offers exceptionally stable handling under a heavy load. Regrettably, some speed and handling agility is sacrificed in the process.

All modern touring bikes come with brazed-on attachments for two or three water bottles and with eyelets for mounting front and rear baggage racks and mudguards. (Mudguards are commonly called fenders.) Even when using the widest tires, a touring bicycle should have ample clearance for mounting plastic mudguards. Though mudguards may spoil the sporty look of your bicycle, they can be lifesavers if you will tour in such perennially rainy areas as

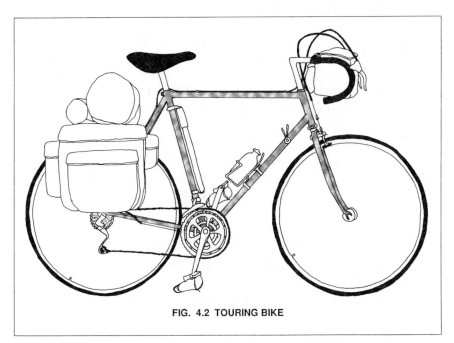

FIG. 4.2 TOURING BIKE

Europe, the British Isles, Ireland, or New Zealand. So make sure that any touring bike you buy will accept mudguards. Better touring bicycles are also equipped with the same powerful cantilever brakes as mountain bicycles. And the triple crankset, standard on all touring bicycles, allows you to climb hills as easily as with a mountain bicycle.

Rims are usually 700 × 32, or 27″ with 1¼″ tires (or optional 1⅜ ″ tires for unpaved roads). Some touring bikes offer the same 26″ wheels and 1½″ tires found on city and mountain bicycles. Gearshift levers may be mounted on the stem, or on the handlebars if desired. And a flat handlebar can be substituted for the usual dropstyle handlebar.

Alternatively, by removing the racks and mudguards, and using slightly lighter tires, your touring bicycle can double as a sports bike.

If you live in, or plan to ride in, hilly and mountainous regions, if you plan to do any extended touring, especially in wet weather, and if you may want to ride on fairly smooth, unpaved roads, a touring bike could be for you. Excellent models are produced by Trek, Cannondale, Raleigh, Miyata, Holdsworth, Claude Butler, and other makers.

All-Terrain Bicycles

The mountain bicycle's ability to conquer terrain that many people would hesitate to even walk on, plus its familiar upright riding position and fat nonskid tires, have attracted thousands of adults who feel intimidated by road bikes that resemble racers. As the beginning adult's most popular bike, the mountain bicycle has taken America by storm.

Other attributes of the mountain bicycle have already been noted in Chapter 1. But all of these merits apply only to the true mountain bike. Right at the start, I recommend that beginners avoid buying a mountain racing bicycle or a city or commuter bike.

Ultralight and designed for fast handling by off-road racers and racing teams, the mountain racing bicycle is a highly specialized race-oriented machine that is usually quite expensive. If you want to try off-road racing, your best bet is to sample it on a regular mountain bike first.

Second, city or commuter bikes (they're the same) are simply slightly cheaper, stripped-down versions of the mountain bicycle with fewer gears and no advantages. They're designed for riding in urban traffic and for commuting on potholed city streets while negotiating gratings and broken glass. A true mountain bike will do all this plus you can use it for off-road riding on weekends and evenings. Thus I recommend newcomers to consider only a bonafide mountain bicycle.

Until recently, mountain bicycles could not be used on indoor trainers, but new models now accept off-road bicycles. Thus you can continue to pedal indoors in bad weather.

The Mountain Bicycle

The mountain bicycle is a durable and versatile machine designed for whipping down dirt roads and for riding on trails littered with rocks and stumps. With its wide, 26″ wheels it is equally at home on pavement, though its heavier 26–30 pound weight and greater rolling resistance cut its speed during highway travel. Nonetheless, by using 1½″ road tires — good on either pavement or dirt roads — you can still cruise the highways at a respectable 10–12 m.p.h. Alternatively, you can use the fat, knobby 1.95″ tire, or the larger tractor-type 2″ tire, for negotiating rocky trails. Before you take your bicycle on any trail, however, make sure that mountain bicycles are permitted and welcome (see Chapter 12 for further information).

FIG. 4.3   MOUNTAIN BIKE

Among features all mountain bikes have in common is a flat or slightly raised handlebar that permits riding in the upright position. The sliding seat post allows the saddle to be dropped several inches at the flip of a lever, permitting the feet to straddle the ground for negotiating rough descents. The combination of three chainrings and six to eight freewheel cogs provides 18–24 wide-ranging gear positions — more than enough to maintain a brisk cadence of 60–90 r.p.m. while pedaling over most terrain. And mountain bikes have powerful cantilever brakes that provide all the stopping ability most riders need.

Despite their high center of gravity, mountain bikes are safe and easy to ride. The handlebar-mounted gear shifters and the large, motorcycle-type brake levers provide instant control. Both front and rear derailleurs can be operated simultaneously, allowing you to jump from first to twenty-first gear within a second.

Frame sizes are smaller than for road bikes, ranging 16½–18–20–22–24″ in size. Most women's mountain bikes have 18–19″ frames. Short chainstays and a fairly steep seat angle place the rider's weight over the rear wheel for superior climbing traction while a longer top tube and a still relatively steep head angle makes for lively and responsive handling. Meanwhile, the large-diameter fork blades with their unmistakable rake provide a smooth, shock-absorbing ride and an overall wheelbase of about 42".

Good Mountain Bikes Don't Have to Be Expensive

Most experts recommend that beginners buy a bike with a wheelbase of at least 42" and with chainstays of at least 17". Also worth knowing is that, for the entry-level adult, mountain bikes priced near the bottom of the average price scale almost all provide surprisingly good handling and riding capability.

While mountain bicycles tend to cost about 20 percent more than road bikes, few beginners need a top-of-the-line model. If you plan to tour, however, check for adequate dropout eyelets and brazed-on attachments for water bottles, touring bags, and racks.

Many riders today use a mountain bicycle with 1½" tires for long-distance highway touring. One advantage is their ability to take to almost any kind of gravel or dirt shoulder should traffic conditions warrant. They are also less susceptible to punctures.

The mountain bicycle is not recommended for fast club or group rides. But for fitness, leisurely club rides, solo day rides, or touring; for climbing hills or mountains; and for any kind of dirt road or off-road travel, the mountain bicycle is hard to beat.

Women's Bicycles

If you're a woman 5'4" in height or under, you may find that a conventional bicycle doesn't fit as well as it should. That's because most conventional frames were designed for men, and women have marked physiological differences.

In comparison to men, women have shorter arms and torsos, smaller hands and feet, narrower shoulders, longer legs, a broader behind, and a wider pelvis. To ride a conventional man's frame, a woman must stretch out, tilting the pelvis forward. This distortion often leads to discomfort in neck, shoulders, and pelvis.

The basic problem is that the top tube is usually too long while components such as brake levers may be too large for women's hands, and crankarms can be too long for a short woman's reach. Sliding the saddle far forward while using the shortest stem extension may help. But it doesn't entirely compensate for a top tube that is nearly an inch too long.

Several manufacturers have overcome this problem by designing bicycles to match a woman's physiology. The top tube is approx-

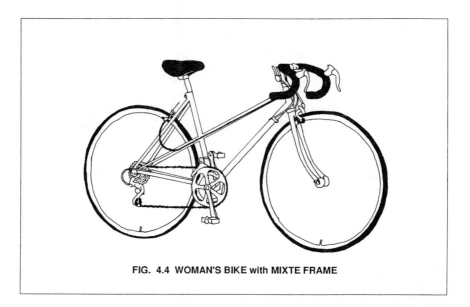

FIG. 4.4 WOMAN'S BIKE with MIXTE FRAME

imately 2 cm shorter than on a conventional bike, and on frames of 19″ or under, components are tailored in proportion. On some extra-small models, either the front wheel, or both the front and rear wheels, may be only 24″ in diameter.

New Women's Models for Every Riding Style

The new women's bikes are available for racing, sports, touring, or mountain bicycling. I recommend that women 5′4″ in height or under seriously consider buying one of these new women's models. The new women's models have diamond frames with a top tube just as on a conventional man's frame.

You should note, though, that these new models differ from the traditional step-through ladies' bicycles in which the top tube is cut away or dropped to form a "ladies' " or mixte frame. The problem with these traditional women's models is that they are not as strong or as stable as a "man's" bicycle, though the mixte frame is a good compromise. Incidentally, the step-through ladies' bicycle will generally not fit a woman taller than 5′8″. Most taller women can ride a conventional bicycle.

Assuming a bicycle fits her, a woman of almost any height can successfully ride a conventional diamond frame. However, if for some reason you prefer a step-through cutaway frame, I recommend trying to locate one that has a mixte type frame.

The new women's bicycles with frames of 19″ or under usually have smaller components including short 165 mm crankarms; small toeclips; a narrow handlebar; compact brake levers; a short stem; and a wide, well-padded saddle designed to accommodate the female pelvis.

Among manufacturers recently specializing in women's bikes is Terry's Precision Bicycles for Women, 1704 Wayne Port Road, Macedon NY 14502 (1–800–289–8379). Other women's road and ATB models have been made by Trek, Centurion, Cannondale, Bridgestone, Nishiki, Panasonic, Fuji, Lotus, Fisher, Raleigh and others.

Tandems

Since the average tandem buyer is aged 45, tandems are designed with the mature adult more in mind. A bicycle built for two equalizes two riders with unequal abilities. A person who enjoys cycling 70 miles a day can cheerfully share a tandem with a partner able to ride only 30 miles. Together they can easily rack up 50 miles. It's a great way for couples to stay active together.

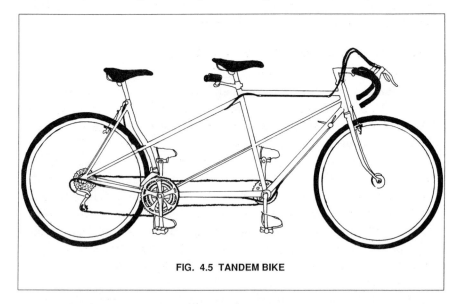

FIG. 4.5 TANDEM BIKE

But sharing a tandem requires a degree of compatibility that some couples simply don't have. For example, the rear rider can't turn around, lean out, or shift weight suddenly. The front rider balances for both, and also does all the steering, braking, and gear shifting. Both riders must learn to start off together and then to pedal in synchronized rhythm. A tandem requires more handling skills; for example, corners must be taken more widely.

Although aerodynamically more efficient, a tandem is slower uphill. Yet it literally rockets downhill, so much so that most tandems require three brakes. A wide gear range is obviously essential. The frame and components are all heavy duty. Thus tandems take longer to build and cost two to three times as much as a solo bike. You may have to wait several months for a stock model to be delivered.

But increasing numbers of tandems are showing up, ridden by couples of every age from yuppies to retirees. Tandem sales are doubling annually. The average age of members of the Tandem Club of America is 45 years. And special tandem rides, events, and tours are held all over the United States.

Santana, the largest maker, produces ten models, seven of which are for touring. Other tandems are made by Schwinn, Burley Design Cooperative, Ritchey USA, and Cannondale, while Fisher Mountain Bikes produces a mountain bike version. Tandems also come in racing, sports, or touring models.

Choosing a tandem as your first bike can be riskier than buying a solo bike. A lot depends on your partner. If you're considering a togetherness bike, try one out first, even if you have to rent a department store tandem. If you anticipate touring abroad, you'll want to know that a tandem is more difficult to ship by plane. And its wheelbase is far too long to fit into your car trunk.

Which Bicycle Shall I Buy?

If you're still uncertain as to which type of bicycle to buy, consider this. Experience shows that mature adults are more likely to take up touring than racing. So let's eliminate a road racer. That leaves a choice between a sports or touring bicycle, and a mountain bike.

Some manufacturers are now producing a hybrid sports-touring bike. The sports-tourer has slightly tighter frame geometry than a standard touring bike along with caliper brakes and a triple crankset. So for a road bike with a drop-type handlebar, a hybrid sports-touring bike is probably the best compromise.

Otherwise, a mountain bike is a fairly safe bet. You can ride it on

highways or on unpaved roads, on day rides or on extensive tours, or
you can ride it around cities and around the park if you want to.

Or if you might prefer a compromise between a mountain and a
touring bike, the road/off-road hybrids became available as this
book was being written. A cross between a road and an off-road
bicycle, the hybrid is a highly versatile machine that combines the
best features of a mountain bike with those of a land cruiser. It looks
like a leaner type of mountain bike with drop-style handlebars, and
it can traverse both pavement and smooth dirt roads or hard-packed
trails. But in its versatility lies its weakness. It is not as good as a
mountain bike on a rough road nor can it equal a road bike on a
highway. Yet for someone who still isn't sure where he or she is
headed in bicycling, the road/off-road hybrid can be a good
compromise.

By now you will have gathered that there is more than one
variety of hybrid. To identify the hybrid you want, ask for a sports-
touring hybrid or a touring-mountain bike hybrid, always naming
the two bicycle types that the hybrid lies between.

Brand Names and Decals

Having by now decided on the type of bicycle you need, you are
probably wondering which brand name you should buy.

Some bicycles and components are still made in Europe. But
today 90 percent of all frames and components are manufactured by
a mere half-dozen companies in Taiwan and Japan. Thus these
manufacturers offer the same technology to virtually all the 75 or so
firms that assemble and sell bicycles on the U.S. market. Many of
these firms simply buy the same generic frames from a manufacturer in the Orient and stick their own brand-name decals on it.
This has led many bicyclists to believe that decals and brand names
have relatively little significance.

Since a bike is the sum of its components, what you should look
for is a bicycle that is *well-built*, not merely one with a well-known
brand name. Quality construction counts more than decals, especially the workmanship in the frame. Today, Taiwan produces top-
quality frames while Japan manufactures high-quality drive-train
and other components. The best built, medium-priced bikes draw
on quality parts from both countries.

If you've read and absorbed this book so far, you should have
formed a good idea of what you want in a bike. Each bike shop
usually carries a limited number of brands so you'll want to visit

several bike shops for a wider comparison. Be sure to check the year of any model you plan to buy. Some bikes may remain unsold on the showroom floor for over a year. Thus a shop may try to sell you a last year's bike that may lack important high-tech advances that are incorporated into the current year's model.

Buy Only from a Quality Adult Bicycle Shop

Try to patronize only stores that offer *adult* bicycles. Most such stores carry only bicycles of dependable quality and your bicycle will be professionally assembled with a free tuneup and alignment provided after 30 days. That's because spokes, cables, bearings, and other components tend to need adjusting after a new bike has been ridden for a month.

Through a bicycle shop you can also arrange a gearing swap, or you can arrange changes in chainrings, crankarms, saddle, handlebars, or virtually anything else. Most bicycle shops also provide their own shop warranty (such as free labor to replace failed parts for 60–90 days after purchase) in addition to the manufacturer's warranty.

Study the manufacturer's warranty carefully. Most guarantee the frame and fork against failure due to faulty workmanship or materials for the life of the bike—but to the original purchaser only. Components are also usually guaranteed for 6–12 months. All guarantees are void if the bicycle is abused or damaged in an accident.

By comparison, department stores usually carry production line bicycles with components of mediocre quality. Frames are usually of small-diameter tubing and parts lack the precision that is needed for smooth functioning. The bikes are then often poorly assembled by inexperienced help. No test rides are allowed, nor are you offered a free tuneup after 30 days. Spare parts are often hard to find, and most quality bike shops refuse to repair production line bicycles.

Sure, you can save some money. But if you've followed this book so far, you will already know better than to buy a department store bike.

How Good Are Mail-order Bicycles?

How about a quality bicycle offered through a mail-order catalog? Here again you can probably save some money. But there is seldom a shop warranty, nor are you offered a free tune-up after 30 days. There is no experienced salesperson to make certain that the bicycle fits you. And to read the specifications in a catalog often requires more experience than most beginners possess.

Buying that Bicycle

In 1990 a no-frills bike of medium quality cost about $400. As the price increased to around $700, so did the quality of frame and components. But $700 was about tops for a medium-quality road bike. To pay more bought only subtle improvements of importance only to the more advanced rider. Mountain bikes cost about 20 percent more.

How about a used bike? What about all those great bikes that adults bought in past years and then stashed away in the garage, never to be used again? If you can find a quality bike in good condition that has obviously had little use, and that can be purchased inexpensively, you can be getting a bargain.

But if it is several years old, a bike won't have recent high-tech advances such as tight geometry, indexed shifting, elliptical chainrings, or a wide gear range. Nonetheless, since quality components are usually put only on a quality frame, the label on a frame can be a good tipoff to the overall quality of an older bike. If the label says something like, "Guaranteed made with Reynolds 531 double butted tubes, forks, and stays," an older road bike might be worth buying—at the right price! Even then, you should have an experienced bicyclist check it out for you before buying.

If your budget is limited, don't plan to spend all of it on the bicycle. You will also need a helmet, gloves, a pump, and a nylon bag to hold tools, tire irons, and two spare tubes plus spare spokes and brake and derailleur cables. You will also need one or two water bottles and cages, and possibly shoes.

Consider what you'll do if it rains. Far too many riders take a chance and go without raingear. A summer thunderstorm can soak an unprotected rider in a few minutes, leaving the rider chilled and shivering and at risk for hypothermia. For the time being, a plastic raincoat or poncho might do. But eventually you may need more dependable raingear. You may also need a larger nylon handlebar or rack bag, and a rear rack. Most bicycle accessories and clothing can be quite expensive unless obtained through a mailorder catalog.

Ensuring a Correct Fit

If your bicycle frame doesn't fit, or if the saddle is wrongly positioned, you can look like a frog on a bicycle. Among the benefits of patronizing a quality bike shop are that you *will* get a bicycle with a frame that fits, and your saddle *will* be correctly positioned.

Frame sizes have already been explained in Chapter 2. To find the minimum frame size you need, divide your height by 3. Thus a 6′ person needs a frame of at least 24″ and a person 6′3″ tall needs a 25″ or 25½″ frame.

To ensure that a particular bike fits, straddle it, wearing the shoes you intend to ride in. With both feet flat on the floor, there should be 1–2″ of clearance between your crotch and the top tube of any road bike. For a mountain bike, the clearance should be 2–3½″.

Bike shop personnel will also adjust the saddle to match your height and body build. Most novice riders position the saddle too low, creating unnecessary stress and pain in the knees. Saddle height is correct when the knees remain slightly bent at the bottom of each stroke (when the ball of the foot is on the pedal in the full-down position). Bike shop personnel will then hold the bike so that you can backpedal. If you rock from side to side, even slightly, the saddle is too high. When adjusting saddle height, at least two inches of the post must remain in the seat tube. Otherwise, you need a longer post.

FIG. 4.6   SADDLE HEIGHT

Saddle height is correct when the knees remain slightly bent at the bottom of each stroke.

To adjust the saddle to the correct height, place your heels on top of the pedal. (If shoes have heels, use your instep.) At the bottom of the pedal stroke, the knee should have only a slight bend. With toeclips, use the underside of the pedal when making this measurement.

Next, you'll be asked to sit on the bicycle with crankarms in the 3 and 9 o'clock position. When the saddle is correctly positioned, the bottom of your knee cap should be directly above the center of the pedal spind'e when in the 3 o'clock (forward) position. Check both sides. Some bike shops drop a plumb line from the bottom of the kneecap of the forward knee. They then adjust the saddle until the plumb line bisects the pedal spindle. If your bike has a slack seat angle (72° rather than 74°) a good mechanic may also adjust the saddle slightly rearward for superior pedaling power.

Adjusting Your Bicycle for the Correct Riding Position

With road bikes, the same plumb line is often used to check a second fore-and-aft saddle adjustment. As you grip the handlebar drops (the part of the handlebar which curves downward closer to

FIG. 4.7   SADDLE POSITION

To check for correct saddle position, turn the pedals to the 9 and 3 o'clock positions, parallel to the ground. When the saddle is correctly positioned, the bottom of your kneecap should be directly above the center of the pedal spindle in the forward (9 o'clock) position.

For an accurate measurement, the ball of the foot must be on the pedal.

the ground), the bike mechanic will suspend the plumb line from the tip of your nose. If the saddle is correctly placed, the plumb should fall approximately one inch in front of the top of your stem. The handlebar itself is then adjusted so that the drops are almost parallel with the ground but facing slightly upward and forward. Meanwhile, the tip of each brake lever is aligned with the flat part of the drops.

The stem is also usually set about one inch below the saddle height. Many racers prefer it still lower while bicycle tourists tend to have the stem higher, the better to view the scenery.

Most bikes are designed for men of average height and build. If you're so tall that there is dangerously little support left for the stem and post, you should consider a frame of 27″.

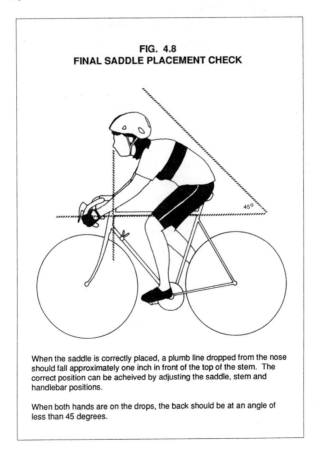

FIG. 4.8
FINAL SADDLE PLACEMENT CHECK

When the saddle is correctly placed, a plumb line dropped from the nose should fall approximately one inch in front of the top of the stem. The correct position can be acheived by adjusting the saddle, stem and handlebar positions.

When both hands are on the drops, the back should be at an angle of less than 45 degrees.

When Steep Geometry Isn't Always Fastest

A common difficulty with correct fit occurs when a rider with unusually long thighs tries to adjust the saddle on a racing or sports bike with very steep angles. With a seat angle of 75° the saddle can seldom be moved sufficiently rearward to allow a rider with long thighs to deliver optimal pedal power to the road. The solution is to buy a bike with angles slack enough so that the saddle can be adjusted further toward the rear to compensate for the long thighs. Thus if you have this body build, a steep-angled frame may not always be synonymous with speed.

To ensure an optimal fit for cleats, and for road racers in general, some shops offer clients a Fit-Kit session at extra cost. Since the fit is racer-oriented, a Fit-Kit session is worthwhile only if you will wear cleats or use clipless pedals.

After riding for a month you will discover if any further adjustments are needed and the bike shop will make these changes without charge during the 30-day tuneup.

If and when you decide to buy a bike, one final adjustment may be needed. If the bike has a kick stand, have the mechanic remove it before you leave the shop. A kick stand frequently causes a bike to fall, or to be blown over, and it adds unnecessary weight.

Experienced riders prevent unsightly frame scratches by leaning their bikes against a tree or post, or by laying them down, so that only the rack stays come in contact with other objects.

CHAPTER 5

Bicycle Care and Repairs

*U*nless you ride with a mechanically-adept companion, on any kind of day ride, club ride, or noncommercial tour you must be prepared to handle the occasional flat tire or broken cable or spoke. In practice this is much simpler than it sounds. Carry basic tools and spares, and learn how to use them, and you seldom need be delayed more than a few minutes.

Care

Check Out Your Bicycle Before Riding

To minimize the chances of a mechanical problem developing during a ride, make these checks before starting out.

Check that the quick-releases are both closed and locked tight.

Check that the crankset and headset are both free of play. As you push the bike forward, squeeze each brake lever in turn.

Check that the wheels are free of side play.

Spin the wheels to check that they are "true" (i.e., not wobbly) and pluck the spokes to check that all are reasonably tight.

Check inflation by pressing the tires between fingers and thumbs for low pressure.

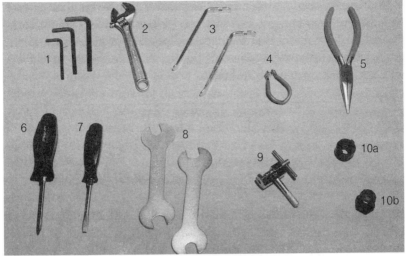

For touring, you should carry a basic tool kit including the items shown here: 1) set of 4-5-6 mm hexagonal wrenches (Allen wrenches); 2) small adjustable wrench; 3) tire irons; 4) spoke wrench; 5) needlenose pliers; 6) Phillips screwdriver; 7) flat-bladed screwdriver; 8) pair of cone wrenches; 9) chain rivet extractor; 10a) freewheel remover (two-prong Suntour model); or 10b) freewheel remover (splined Shimano model). For day rides, you should carry at least the first seven items. It is also advisable to carry the following spare parts: tube, rim tape, two spokes, rear brake cable, and rear derailleur cable.

For day rides you need a small basic tool kit that includes a set of 4-5-6 mm L-shaped hexagonal wrenches (often called Allen wrenches), a small adjustable wrench, a pair of needlenose pliers, two aluminum tire irons, a spoke wrench, and a Phillips and a flat-bladed screwdriver. For touring you also need a pair of cone wrenches, a chain rivet extractor, and a freewheel remover, if you have a freewheel. Most bike shops carry compact, lightweight tool kits that contain all these tools in a handy pouch. You should also carry at least one spare tube, a spare rim tape, two spare spokes for each size used, one spare rear brake cable, and one spare rear derailleur cable.

If riding a mountain bike or tandem, make sure the spare cables are tandem length. For extended touring you should carry at least three spare tubes, several additional spokes, and a tube patch kit. I also carry a six-inch length of old tire (minus the bead), which can be used as a patch inside a tire should it split. On a tour I also carry a small can of spray or drip oil and a crank bolt wrench.

Finally, I always carry a frame pump on the bike. For Presta valves, get one with a thumb lock pumphead that fits securely on the valve. Such a pump will inflate tubes to about 90 pounds per square inch (p.s.i.). You may also like to have a floor pump at home that will inflate tubes to 125 p.s.i. or more. Make sure any pump you buy fits the valves you are using.

Unfortunately, this isn't a repair manual so I can't tell you step by step exactly how to change a tube or replace a broken cable or spoke. There are several good basic bike repair books on the market that go into much greater detail. But here are a few tips on how to handle minor repairs that may occur while out riding.

Changing a Tube

If you have a flat tire while riding, pump both brakes to slow and stop the bike. The flat tire itself will also slow you down. Should the front tire go flat, the bike will become harder to steer, and you must keep the handlebars straight while braking. Once you have stopped, get off the road and find a grassy, shady spot.

Release the brake on the wheel with the flat. If the front tire is punctured, trip the quick-release and remove the wheel. If it's the rear wheel, move the chain onto the smallest cog and chainring. Remove all bags, bottles, etc. and turn the bike upside down. Then remove the wheel. (With some bikes, the rear wheel can be removed without inverting the bike.)

Look for a visible thorn, nail, or piece of glass. Remove it from the tire in one piece if you can. Lay the wheel down and use the tire irons to carefully remove the bead of one side of the tire from the

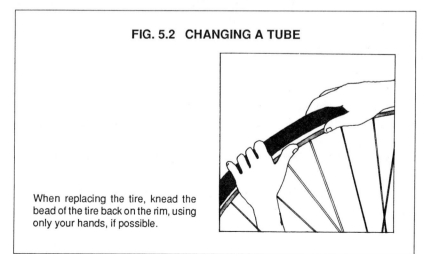

FIG. 5.2 CHANGING A TUBE

When replacing the tire, knead the bead of the tire back on the rim, using only your hands, if possible.

wheel. Then remove the tube completely from the rim. Run your fingertips around inside the tire, feeling for any protruding sharp points. If you find one, try to remove the thorn, nail, etc., from the outside. Do not leave any sharp object inside the tire.

Pull the tire to one side and check that the rim tape covers the spokeheads. Insert a new tube. Pump in a small quantity of air, just enough to keep the tube extended inside the tire. Then, using your hands, start at the valve and knead the bead of the tire back on the rim. If the last few inches of tire absolutely refuses to go back on the rim, make sure that the beads on the opposite side of the tire have dropped into the deepest part of the rim. If that doesn't work, you may have to use very gentle pressure with a tire iron to finally get the tire back on. Take great care not to pinch the tube between rim and tire. (When a tire is this difficult to replace, it often indicates that the tire is not compatible with the rim.)

Pinch the sidewalls between fingers and thumbs all the way around the circumference of the rim to release the tube should it be caught. Inflate the tube lightly. Then deflate it. Run your fingers and thumbs around the tire, pinching the sidewalls together once more. Then inflate the tire hard and replace the wheel on the bike.

Squeeze the air out of the punctured tube and carry it in your bag. You do not need to patch a tube on the road. Repair it either when you reach home, or at the end of the day's ride if on a tour.

Rather than buy a tube patch kit I purchase a dozen 1¼" diameter patches from a bike shop plus some rubber cement, sandpaper, and a yellow china-marking pencil. The pencil is invaluable for marking the location of the puncture, and the larger 1¼" patches enhance your chances of sealing the leak. If your tubes are not made of butyl, you may require special patches.

Replacing Broken Cables

Replacing a broken cable is something you can learn only by watching it being done. However, you can spare yourself some grief by buying spare cables that have the correct-sized lug on one end. The other end should be neatly cut and either brazed or soldered, or else sealed with a nipple, so that it cannot unravel. When threading it through the housing, rotate the cable in the opposite direction to that in which it is wound. Unless you have a pair of special cyclist's cable cutters, never buy a cable that has a different-shaped lug at each end. You are expected to cut off the undesired lug, but without special cutters you will not make a clean cut and the cable will not thread through the housing on your bike.

If you have a broken brake or front derailleur cable, you can probably manage to finish your ride for the day. But if the rear derailleur cable goes, you must usually stop and replace it.

FIG. 5.3 SPECIAL CABLE CUTTERS

Replacing a Broken Spoke

Should a spoke break on the front wheel, or on the left side of the rear wheel, replacing it is usually a simple operation that can be done in a few minutes without removing the wheel from the bicycle.

On the other hand, if during a day ride, a spoke breaks on the freewheel (right) side of the rear wheel, consider returning to your car or heading for a bike shop, if one is nearby. The reason for this advice is that to thread a new spoke on the right side of the rear wheel necessitates first removing the freewheel or freehub cogs. On a tour, assuming you are carrying a freewheel remover, you can remove the freewheel by using a large wrench or vise at a repair garage. All this, of course, refers to a conventional freewheel.

How about a freehub?

To unlock a freehub and remove the cogs, you have 3 options: (1) carry a rather bulky tool called a chainwhip; (2) carry a mini-whip tool called a cassette cracker; or (3) if neither is available, you can, in an emergency, block the smallest cog with a screwdriver and put weight on the crank to unscrew it. To make option 3 clearer: above the rear dropouts, where the chain and seat stays meet, almost every frame has a small triangular opening. Through this triangle, you can insert a screwdriver so that it lies between two teeth of the smallest cog. This effectively prevents the cog from turning. However, it should be used only as a last resort because it can slightly damage the enamel finish in the triangle area.

A Cassette Cracker does essentially the same thing but without risk of damaging the bike's finish. New as this was written, cassette crackers are becoming widely available. However, current models would not fit Hyperglide cogs.

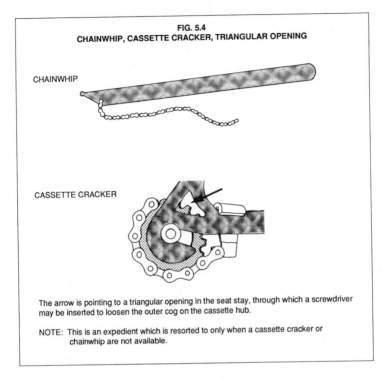

FIG. 5.4
CHAINWHIP, CASSETTE CRACKER, TRIANGULAR OPENING

CHAINWHIP

CASSETTE CRACKER

The arrow is pointing to a triangular opening in the seat stay, through which a screwdriver may be inserted to loosen the outer cog on the cassette hub.

NOTE: This is an expedient which is resorted to only when a cassette cracker or chainwhip are not available.

To carry out options 2 or 3, move the chain onto the largest cog and onto the smallest chainring. Place the cranks at 3 and 9 o'clock. Attach the mini-whip or screwdriver. Now place your full weight on the forward pedal. The entire rear wheel assembly should rotate while the small cog, prevented from moving by the mini-whip or screwdriver, begins to unscrew. Once loosened, the small cog can be easily unscrewed and the cogs removed from the freehub cassette.

If a spoke is broken anywhere but close to or inside the nipple, twist the broken spoke and unscrew it out of the nipple. Remove the other broken piece of spoke from the wheel hub. Thread a new spoke in its place. You may have to bend it a bit in the process. Insert the threaded spoke end into the nipple and tighten with a spoke wrench.

If the spoke is broken too close to the nipple, partially remove the tube and tire so that you can replace the nipple with a new one. Then tighten the spoke and replace the tube and tire.

Should a spoke break within an hour or so of the end of your day's ride, consider nursing the bike along for the rest of the way, taking care not to break a second spoke. You may have to release a brake to do so.

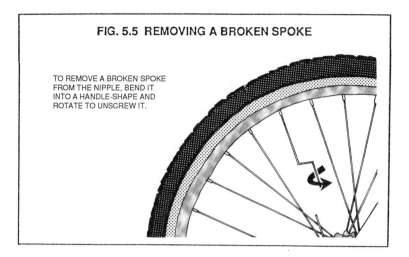

FIG. 5.5 REMOVING A BROKEN SPOKE

TO REMOVE A BROKEN SPOKE
FROM THE NIPPLE, BEND IT
INTO A HANDLE-SHAPE AND
ROTATE TO UNSCREW IT.

Other Repairs

Among less common but easily remedied roadside adjustments you can handle yourself are these.

The chain skips a tooth on the rear cog every few seconds. This is due to a tight spot in the chain. Place the chain on the middle chainring and the smallest cog. Slowly rotate the chain backward by hand while you watch the rear derailleur pulleys, where the tight spot can be seen.

Move the tight spot to midway between the crankset and the rear derailleur. Using both hands, hold the chain by its sideplates on each side of the tight spot and flex it vigorously. This usually corrects the problem.

The rear derailleur does not drop back onto the smallest cog when you release the gearshift lever. This can usually be remedied by adjusting the screw marked "H" (for high gear) on the rear derailleur counterclockwise or outward, using a Phillips screwdriver or a pocket knife.

The chain overshifts and drops between the largest cog and the rear wheel spokes. This can usually be remedied by adjusting the screw marked "L" (for low gear) on the rear derailleur. Turn the screw clockwise or inward.

In contrast, if the chain refuses to go all the way onto the largest cog, turn the screw counterclockwise or outward. When adjusting derailleurs, usually only a quarter- or half-turn of the adjusting screw is necessary.

CHAPTER 6

How Bicycling Helps You Stay Younger and Live Longer

*B*icycling is not only good for the heart and lungs. It also creates a sense of intense and lasting joy.

Several studies have shown that among the many benefits of bicycling regularly is its ability to beat depression. In fact, the past decade has witnessed an explosion of research findings suggesting that regular rhythmic exercise can benefit every part of the body right down to our cells.

Most adults initially take up bicycling to improve their fitness. Those who stay with it often achieve dramatic improvements in just a few weeks. Frequently they go on to ride centuries, or to go on long tours, or to compete in races. But all too many give up within a short time and never ride again.

What makes the difference?

Four essential factors govern success in cycling: (1) having the right bike with the right gears — a topic we've already covered; (2) eating the right foods to fuel your body's energy needs; (3) becoming a competent rider so that you can keep the pedals spinning at a cadence of 60–90 r.p.m. in all kinds of terrain; and (4) bicycling regularly so that your body learns to mobilize the energy you need to build stamina.

Assuming you follow all four principles, exactly what health benefits can you expect?

To demonstrate the many and varied benefits of rhythmic exercise such as bicycling, I drew on recommendations by such leading health advisory agencies as the American Heart Association, the National Cancer Society, the National Academy of Sciences, the Pritikin Institutes for Longevity, and the various National Institutes of Health. To these I added the findings of such recent large-scale studies as the Seven Countries Study, the Paffenbarger Study of 17,000 Harvard alumnae, the Framingham Study, the Lipid Research Clinic's mortality followup study, and work done at the Center for Exercise Sciences, University of Florida, Gainesville.

Putting together their combined findings and recommendations reveals this overall picture of bicycling's benefits.

Bicycling Cuts Risk of Heart Disease in Half

Rhythmic activities, like bicycling, that use the body's large muscles, are also known as *aerobic exercise*. Numerous studies have revealed that regular aerobic exercise produces exceptional physical benefits, including improved oxygen uptake and cardiac efficiency. It lowers pulse rate and blood pressure and reduces risk of death from heart disease by more than 50 percent.

Lars-Göran Ekeleund, Ph.D., author of the 8½-year Lipid Research Clinic's mortality followup study, also speculates that regular exercise may reduce blood platelet aggregation, thereby lowering risk of the clumping that frequently triggers a heart attack.

The rhythmic exercise of bicycling appears to boost immunity and cut the risk of certain types of cancer. For example, a study at Harvard University School of Public Health showed that sedentary women have 2.5 times greater risk of breast cancer than women who practice a regular form of exercise such as bicycling.

Bicycling is also one of the best weight-loss exercises. By pedaling at 15 m.p.h. for 9 hours a week, a 120 pound woman will lose one pound and a 150 pound man will lose 1.3 pounds. Keep this up, and in six months the average woman could typically lose 26 pounds and the average man 34 pounds. This loss rate can be doubled by changing to a diet low in fat and high in complex carbohydrates.

Get High Naturally

Thirty minutes after beginning to bicycle, clouds of endorphin are released in the brain. Endorphin, a natural opiate and pain-killer, binds onto receptors in the right hemisphere to induce a euphoric high. Acting as a natural tranquilizer, it elevates mood for up to 24 hours. In the process, stress hormones are dissipated, anxiety and depression fade away, and a deep sense of physical and emotional relaxation begins soon after exercise has ceased.

Undoubtedly because bicycling is an enjoyable exercise, it brings health rewards sooner than some other forms of exercise. Beginners are often amazed at how far and how fast they can ride after only a few weeks of practice. Each time you ride faster and farther, you experience an overwhelming feeling of mastery and success.

Retard the Aging Process

Over 100 major studies have also confirmed that exercises like bicycling, when regularly maintained, can clearly slow the aging process, and may even reverse it. For instance, sedentary adults consistently lose 1 percent of their oxygen (aerobic) capacity each year. Additionally, they experience a steadily diminishing capacity of the heart to pump blood. But studies by Michael Pollock, Ph.D., of the Center for Exercise Sciences, University of Florida, have revealed that people over 30 who adopt a regular exercise such as bicycling, can *increase* their aerobic capacity by 15–30 percent within a relatively short time.

Bicycling regularly keeps the body in shape, gives improved definition to all muscles, and creates a firm, athletic body and a greatly improved appearance. It also increases sexual vigor and improves the quality of sleep.

In another large and well-controlled study, Ralph Paffenbarger, Ph.D., of Stanford University School of Medicine found that up to a certain point, increased amounts of rhythmic exercise can reduce risk of mortality by 40 percent and, at the same time, add 10–20 years to one's life expectancy. Within limits, this means that the more you exercise, the longer you are likely to live.

Based on the number of calories consumed by exercise, I estimate that in bicycling the limit would be to ride about 125 miles per week. Up to that point, the more miles you ride the greater the health benefits. By cycling 125 miles per week at a reasonably brisk pace you can statistically reduce your risk of dying in any one year by approximately 40 percent. But after pedaling a total of 125 miles in a week, the health benefits of additional bicycling begin to taper off.

Diet and Exercise Work Together

All the benefits mentioned so far have been attributed to exercise alone. But when a diet low in fat and protein and high in complex carbohydrates is added, both exercise and diet work synergistically to more than double the benefits that either could produce alone.

If you've taken up bicycling merely to try and lower your cholesterol, you may be disappointed. Many bicyclists erroneously believe that exercise protects them against the hazards of eating high-risk, fatty foods. This is only partially true.

Exercise alone does help to lower the level of triglycerides (fatty acids) in the bloodstream. It also tends to lower the level of LDL (low-density lipoprotein — the "bad" cholesterol). And it very definitely does raise the level of HDL (high-density lipoprotein — the "good" cholesterol).

Yet exercise alone does little to reduce the overall level of serum cholesterol.

This was borne out by a 1984 study of U.S. Olympic bicycle racers at the Grand Forks Nutrition Center of the U.S. Department of Agriculture. Researchers discovered that on a diet high in saturated fats, the serum cholesterol level of the racing cyclists remained high regardless how much they exercised. But when they reduced their intake of saturated fats, their serum cholesterol levels declined by an average 40 percent.

This classic study is one of many to confirm that exercise alone will not lower the serum cholesterol level if a diet high in saturated fats continues to be eaten. But when exercise and diet are combined, results can be significant.

Saturated Fats Shorten Life

While cholesterol is no longer regarded as the chief culprit in causing heart disease, we should not underestimate its danger. Nowadays, however, saturated fat is regarded as the prime villain. Whether of vegetable or animal origin, saturated fat can boost the serum cholesterol level up to 5 times as much as does dietary cholesterol. At the same time, saturated fat raises the level of LDL in the bloodstream.

This doesn't mean it's safe to eat cholesterol. Whether or not you bicycle, intake of both cholesterol and saturated fat should be kept to a minimum. This translates into significantly reducing the number of calories consumed as fat.

A diet high in fat causes overproduction of natural body cholesterol by the liver. This increases the amount of body fat. As body fat
increases, LDL rises and HDL drops, heightening risk of a heart
attack or stroke. Several hundred studies have also incriminated a
high-fat diet, and a high level of body fat, with increased risk of
several types of cancer.

Because they believe that the average American will never lower
his or her calorie intake from fat to less than 30 percent of the diet,
most doctors and health advisory agencies have settled for recommending that Americans cut fat intake from 40 percent to only 30
percent of the diet while keeping the serum cholesterol level at 200
mg/dl or below.

While they may be a step in the right direction for the general
public, these levels are inadequate for anyone who wants to achieve
a high level of fitness and wellness through bicycling.

Eating for Energy and Health

Most sports doctors and others who are nutritionally oriented
recommend much lower levels of dietary fat. Years ago, the late
Nathan Pritikin recommended an 80-10-10 diet, which translates
into 80 percent of calories from complex carbohydrates, 10 percent
from fat, and 10 percent from protein.

BIKECENTENNIAL PHOTO

Touring cyclists enjoy a hearty breakfast in Idaho. "Eat before you're hungry,
drink before you're thirsty, rest before you're tired," is a commonly heard piece
of advice for cyclists.

Since then, thousands of successful athletes have found that fat and animal protein are poor sources of energy. The best source of energy for long bicycle rides, or for any kind of physical exertion, is complex carbohydrates, namely fresh, unprocessed fruits, vegetables, whole grains, legumes, nuts, and seeds in as close to their natural state as possible. Many top athletes today have become strict vegetarians. And scores of leading bicycle racers load up on complex carbohydrates for several days before a race.

Combine an 80-10-10 diet with a regular bicycling exercise program and you can attain an amazingly high level of fitness, stamina, and health in a very short time. It's not unusual for a cyclist to drop his or her cholesterol level by 50 mg/dl during the first month. Many adults who have combined bicycling with a really low-fat diet have dropped their serum cholesterol to 140 mg/dl in just a few weeks. By replacing fat and animal protein with complex carbohydrates, they have achieved exceptional levels of energy, stamina, and endurance.

Foods to Avoid

Foods to eliminate include: all fatty meats, beef fat and lard, whole-milk dairy products (especially cream, ice cream, butter, and cheese), eggs, poultry skin, and saturated shortening. Tropical oils like palm or palm kernel or coconut oil are also taboo, as are the many commercial mixes and baked goods that contain these saturated vegetable oils. These include nondairy creamers and coffee lighteners, nondairy sour cream, and all vegetable shortenings made from tropical oils. All fried foods and commercial popcorn should also be eliminated.

Be careful of any processed or commercially prepared foods. The majority contain eggs or tropical oils or polyunsaturated fats. Once recommended as a substitute for saturated fats, polyunsaturated oils such as safflower, sunflower, corn, or soy oil have been found to lower the "good" HDL along with the "bad" LDL cholesterol. Furthermore, the high proportion of linoleic acid in polyunsaturated fat is believed to suppress immunity and to increase risk of cancer and gallstones.

The One Diet that Does It All

Far safer than either saturated fats or polyunsaturated oils are monounsaturates such as olive oil or canola oil. However, naturally occurring polyunsaturated fats contained in avocados, nuts, seeds,

whole grains, and legumes are considered totally safe when consumed by eating these foods. Together, these sources of safe fat can
more than meet any dietary lipid needs.

It should come as no surprise, really, that the foods that provide
bicyclists with the greatest amounts of energy and stamina are the
same foods that work best to reduce risk of heart disease, cancer,
and other killer diseases. Together, a diet low in fat and animal
protein, and high in complex carbohydrates, when combined with
regular bicycling, enables one to swiftly reach the highest attainable
levels of fitness and health.

Medical literature shows that there is no upper age limit at which
these benefits cease to occur. Bicycling plus sound nutrition will
produce startling results at any age. And bicycling is an exercise that
can be continued safely until very late in life.

High-Risk Foods Can Impair Your Performance

How about people who stay fit by bicycling but who continue to
eat a high-risk diet? Unfortunately, some of the benefits of
bicycling—particularly those pertaining to reduced risk of heart
attack and stroke—can be offset by eating foods high in fats and
animal protein. This caveat applies also to foods high in refined
carbohydrates such as sugar and white flour.

When you watch bicyclists gulping down soda drinks along with
doughnuts, cookies, and cinnamon rolls at roadside stops, one can
only speculate at how much overall benefit they are gaining from
the ride.

All too many mature riders have discovered the hard way that
even moderate amounts of sugar, fat, and animal protein visibly
impair their physical performance—so much so that many bicyclists
prefer to carry their own health snacks in their handlebar bags
rather than rely on finding anything safe and nutritious at roadside
stops.

Good Fuel Foods

Complex carbohydrates in the form of vegetable starches, as well
as fruit sugars, are the food compounds preferred by the body to fuel
all forms of exercise. Fat and animal protein break down too slowly
to provide much energy. One of the main reasons why millions of
Americans are listless and fatigued is because they eat too few
complex carbohydrates.

For the first two hours of a bicycle ride, your energy is supplied by glycogen, a starch stored in the muscles and liver. After riding for two hours or more, these glycogen reserves are depleted and the muscles begin to draw on glucose, a sugar in the bloodstream. Unless replenished by complex carbohydrates, these glucose reserves can soon be used up. When this happens a bicyclist begins to feel listless and fatigued.

While riding, one's glucose supply can be constantly replenished by eating a snack, or having a light meal, about every two hours. During century rides, and long all-day rides, it's vitally important to eat lightly and often. A commonly heard piece of bicycling advice is: "Eat before you're hungry, drink before you're thirsty, rest before you're tired."

You should always carry a snack on any fast-paced ride of over two hours. Since women have smaller muscle mass for storing glycogen, women may need to eat sooner and more often than men riders.

Among the best snacks are bananas and oranges (which replace potassium lost through sweating); figs and dates; whole-grain bagels, muffins, fig bars, and oatmeal cookies; whole-grain bread spread with pure peanut butter; sunflower seeds and raisins; and trail mix or gorp (Good Old Raisins and Peanuts). You can make your own gorp from seeds, nuts, raisins, and whole-grain cereals.

Try to avoid snacking on refined carbohydrates such as candy bars or concoctions of sugar, fat, and white flour. These foods boost the blood sugar level briefly but fail to sustain it long enough to prevent hypoglycemia (low blood sugar) and insulin imbalance. Complex carbohydrates promote much greater glycogen synthesis than do refined carbohydrates, besides which, they are filled with health-building fiber and nutrients.

Complex carbohydrates should also be the basis for your regular meals. To become a high-energy person, build meals around fruits like bananas and cantalopes; vegetables of all kinds; whole-grain breads and pasta; cereals like brown rice, oatmeal, shredded wheat, muesli, grits, millet, or other cereals free of sweeteners; tubers like potatoes, sweet potatoes, and parsnips; and beans of all kinds, especially soybeans. Sunflower seeds and nuts are great for dessert or snacks.

To maximize glycogen storage before an upcoming ride, eat more vegetables and grains and less fat, sugar, salt, and animal protein.

For decades Americans have been obsessed with getting enough protein. According to George M. Blackburn, M.D., Ph.D., associate professor of surgery at Harvard Medical School, most of us eat 2½–3 times as much protein as the body needs. Through overloading the kidneys with protein-breakdown products, renal disease has become increasingly common. In reality, only 6–8 percent of our daily calorie intake needs to be in the form of protein. Most Americans get 15 percent of their calories from protein, and many get much more.

Since meat and other forms of animal protein are high in fat and calories, protein from vegetable sources is preferred. Beans, nuts, seeds, whole grains, and many vegetables supply a variety of amino acids from which complete protein is readily formed. Nor, as many bicyclists believe, does animal protein build up muscle. To build muscles you need exercise, not protein.

Small amounts of very lean meat, fish, or white poultry meat together with nonfat plain yogurt, low-fat cottage cheese, and skim milk are among acceptable low-fat sources of whole protein.

To eat safely in restaurants while bicycling, I usually order a large bowl of oatmeal or grits for breakfast and add fresh fruit that I bring in myself. Vegetable soup with whole-grain bread, salads or salad bar items without dressings, lean meats, baked fish or chicken, pasta without cheese, plain baked potatoes, and bean dishes are among the safer items to order. Some ethnic restaurants serve a variety of meals low in fat. When touring alone, however, I often buy fresh produce at the local supermarket and prepare my own salads or other meals of raw fruits, vegetables, whole-grain bread or corn tortillas in the motel. Or I eat picnic-style outdoors.

What to Put in Your Water Bottle

Water is probably the most common beverage carried by bicyclists. But many also fill their water bottles with sports drinks. Bearing names like Gatorade, Max, Exceed, or Body-Fuel, approximately 8–10 percent of these sports drinks consist of glucose polymers, which are large starchy molecules designed to replenish the body's glycogen reserves. They are also fortified with other essential nutrients and minerals that are lost through sweating. Some studies indicate that these sports drinks can improve bicycling performance by 5–15 percent. Many nutritionists, however, consider these sports drinks unnecessary under normal conditions, believing that drinking plenty of water and eating sensibly are adequate unless unusually strenuous exercise or extremely hot weather is involved.

Most bicyclists carry two large water bottles in hot weather and the majority take a long swig every 15 minutes. Under hot riding conditions, you can easily consume the contents of one large water bottle each hour—and more if it's humid. If you have to cover a long, waterless distance during hot weather, you can carry additional water in a pannier bag. At all costs, you must avoid becoming dehydrated.

Caffeine is also best avoided. Although it provides a temporary lift, caffeine encourages fluid loss through urination. Cola drinks and tea also contain appreciable amounts of caffeine. A heavy caffeine intake may diminish your performance quite noticeably.

A Medical Checkup Before Starting to Bicycle

Although the risk of not starting to exercise is a thousand times greater than any risk involved in starting to exercise, nonetheless, most authorities recommend that you have a medical checkup before beginning a bicycling program. If you are over 30 and overweight or sedentary, a smoker or a steady drinker, take prescription medication regularly, or have a history of heart disease, hypertension, or any other chronic disease or dysfunction that might be adversely affected by bicycling, you will probably be given a stress test. This consists of an electrocardiogram while running on a treadmill or pedaling a stationary bicycle.

Thousands of people who formerly relied on prescription drugs to stay alive have been able to get off drugs entirely through bicycling. If you are on prescription drugs for hypertension or for any other reason, you may—with your physician's cooperation—be able to gradually reduce the dosage, and eventually to get off drugs entirely as the benefits of bicycling replace the need for medication.

CHAPTER 7

Secrets of Successful Bicycling

To realize the health benefits of bicycling you must learn to spin the pedals at 60–90 r.p.m. or more under almost all conditions. Although that implies becoming a competent bicyclist, all it takes really is to learn the following basic skills:

      Starting, braking and stopping

      Riding proficiently

      Cornering

      Shifting gears

      Climbing and descending hills

Starting to Ride

Never mount a modern lightweight bicycle by putting one foot on the pedal and kicking off before you get astride it. This can wrench the frame and it won't work with toeclips.

Instead, stand astride the bicycle with one foot on the ground. Insert the other foot into the pedal and toeclip. Press down on the pedal to gain momentum. Then quickly, as the other crankarm reaches the full-up position, place the sole on the rear edge of the pedal so that it turns upright and lets you slip your toe into the toeclip. Modern weighted and clipless pedals make it all much easier.

To accelerate quickly, stand up from the saddle and place your full weight first on one pedal, then on the other. Practice this in a traffic-free place until you can do it confidently without weaving from side to side.

Once started, you must be able to ride straight without wobbling. If you can't do this yet, the solution is to keep riding until the brain builds the necessary neural pathways to correct your balance. You can do this most safely on a bicycle path or anywhere else free of vehicles. Do not attempt to ride on streets or roads until you are able to ride straight.

Braking and Stopping

You'll quickly discover that the front brake has more stopping power than the rear. Avoid applying the front brake suddenly, as it could grab or lock and throw you over the handlebars. You can minimize this possibility by sliding back in the saddle as you apply the front brake.

To stop quickly, apply both brakes together. Assuming there is ample room to stop, use the rear brake only.

As you stop, slide forward off the saddle and remove one foot from the toeclip, placing it on the ground. Most riders place their right foot on the ground. If you stop beside a curb, you can place the right foot on the curb without sliding off the saddle.

Riding Proficiently

To ride long distances without fatigue you must learn to ride in the most efficient posture. Most of what I'm going to say concerns riding a road bike with drop-style handlebars. But much of the advice is just as applicable to a mountain bicycle.

Many beginners ride with their shoulders hunched up and with the neck, back, arms, and hands held rigid and tense. Holding the upper body tense not only wastes energy but hinders you in making subtle steering changes.

Instead, keep the body above the waist loose and relaxed. Keep the back as straight as possible *but lower your shoulders.* Keep the elbows flexed and hold the handlebars lightly with your fingers. Only when you stand up from the saddle need you grasp the handlebars more firmly. Use your arms and hands like a jockey riding a racehorse.

On a *road bike,* the angle of your back should be about 45° to the *road*. In this position, only about half your weight is on the saddle. Approximately 45 percent is supported by your legs as you press down on the pedals, and about 5 percent is borne by your arms.

Keep the balls of your feet on the center of the pedals, a position guaranteed by having toeclips and straps. As you begin each pedal downstroke, push the lower leg forward and add power from the thigh. Ease up on pressure as the foot approaches the bottom of the stroke. Although it isn't essential, you can increase pedaling power by pulling up with your leg during the upstroke. To do this your toeclip strap must be tight, or you must use clipless pedals.

In any event, avoid chopping at the pedals with your feet. Instead, swivel the ankle to add power to your pedaling. In this way you can maintain a smooth and fluid pedaling motion.

Change Your Riding Position Frequently

To prevent stiffness and fatigue, vary your riding position every few minutes. The advantage of drop-type handlebars is that they offer at least three different hand positions. You can place the hands on top of the handlebar. You can place the heels of your hands on the brake lever hoods. Or you can place your hands down on the drops.

Going down on the drops provides a streamlined position that can cut wind resistance. The bent-over posture also increases muscle power to the pedals. But leaning forward also stretches the back, extends the spine and — although it's hard to believe — allows a greater intake of air into the lungs.

You should always ride in the crouched-over position, with your hands on the drops, while pedaling into a headwind.

At every opportunity while coasting during long rides, you should relax by standing up on the pedals and flexing the back. You should also frequently flutter the fingers, flex the elbows, and deliberately drop and relax the shoulders.

Riding in a Paceline

Whenever two or more riders are facing a headwind, both can make better time by working together in a paceline. This simply means riding in single file, one behind the other. This is standard practice in racing and is described in Chapter 15 under "How to Ride in a Pack." Look there for other helpful advice.

But bicyclists frequently trade pace, as it's called, even when touring or during a day ride. The front rider works harder to overcome wind resistance while the other riders trail closely behind, each in the slipstream of the rider ahead. In this way, all except the leader can reduce pedaling effort by 15–20 percent.

Riders should agree on how long each shall remain in the lead position. Usually it's for one minute, or for 0.25 miles on their computer, or for 100 pedal revolutions. After that, the leader turns left and drops back to the rear of the paceline while the rider behind becomes the new leader. When riders in the paceline are unevenly matched, a weaker rider may stay in the lead for only 75 revolutions while a stronger rider may stay up front for 125 revolutions.

On an average highway, up to 6 riders can ride in a paceline without inconveniencing traffic. If you ride in a paceline, always look back and check for overtaking cars before turning out and dropping back to the rear.

Cornering Correctly

Before making a turn, slow down to a safe speed. Always try to make the widest turn possible, traffic permitting, and avoid getting near a curb. Lean inward in the direction of the turn. And for better traction and stability, slide back a bit towards the rear of the saddle.

When freewheeling around any bend or curve, always raise the inside pedal and lower the outside pedal. This prevents the inside pedal from possibly touching the ground or curb. It's also best to avoid shifting gears during a turn as it could cause an imbalance.

Keep Those Pedals Spinning Briskly

Spinning the pedals briskly in lower gears at a cadence of 60–90 r.p.m. or more is the secret of successful bicycling. If you ride in higher gears and fail to maintain a brisk pedaling cadence, you may experience fatigue, muscle strain, and knee problems. I've found that almost every novice who experiences knee problems is actually grinding away in big gears and pedaling at a cadence of 50 r.p.m. or less.

By spinning at 80 r.p.m. instead, you reduce the pressure on pedals and knees by almost half at each revolution.

The trick is to get into a pedaling rhythm you can stay with (in the 60–90 r.p.m. range or higher) and then maintain that same rhythm by shifting gears to match changing conditions of wind and terrain. The closer you are to 90 r.p.m. rather than 60 r.p.m., the better. Fast spinning prevents knee and joint problems. Almost all touring riders stay within a range of 65–95 r.p.m., and they maintain a steady, even style.

If spinning feels strange or difficult, first get used to riding at 60 r.p.m. Then gradually get used to spinning faster, in 5 r.p.m. increments, until you feel comfortable above 80 r.p.m.

Only by riding briskly on a multi-geared bicycle with a wide range of gears can you anticipate all the health benefits described earlier. You can't spin the pedals briskly enough on a 3- or 5-speed bicycle, or on one with a narrow gear range. And you must cycle where you can make long, uninterrupted rides. Riding on bike paths or around the neighborhood bestows few health or fitness benefits.

Shifting Gears—Smart, Fast, Crisp

To shift gears on a derailleur bicycle you must keep pedaling. During the moment of actual shifting, ease up on pedal pressure. Known as soft-pedaling, this technique means that you maintain only enough pressure to keep the pedals spinning. Immediately after you click into gear, resume the pressure. However, on bicycles equipped with the Hyperglide shifting system, you can shift the rear derailleur under full pedaling load, while the Superglide system lets you shift chainrings also while under full pedaling load.

Unlike a 3-speed, you cannot shift derailleur gears once the bicycle has stopped. Nor should you ever backpedal while shifting derailleur gears.

Among recent innovations are combined gearshift and brake levers mounted on the handlebars side by side. However, most road bikes still have the gearshift levers on the downtube while mountain bikes have a single lever on each side of the handlebar. On a road bike you must remove one hand from the handlebar to shift. Practice shifting the levers while keeping your eyes on the road. You will soon be able to shift by feel without looking down.

It's OK to glance down at the drive train for a second. Most riders have to, from time to time, to check on which chainring and cogs they are actually in. But get your eyes back on the road as soon as you can.

With downtube shifters you can shift only one lever at a time. For a double shift you must first move the left lever to shift the chainring, then move the right lever to shift the cog. Each rider has his or her own preference for accomplishing this. Some use the right hand to move both levers. Others use the right hand for the right lever and the left hand for the left lever. With a small frame or large tubes you may have to use the latter system. On a mountain bike you can shift both levers simultaneously by flicking your thumbs.

Indexed shifting makes all gear changing easier and smoother. Usually only the rear derailleur is indexed. But it allows you to click into exactly the right cog setting immediately. By comparison, with friction shifting, you must shift by feel and it's all too easy to overshift or undershift. Although you can adjust for this immediately, it still means that friction shifting takes slightly longer.

Mastering the Basics

In Chapter 3 I recommended using a crankset with triple chainrings. If you have three chainrings, use the smallest for climbing hills or riding into headwinds, the middle chainring for generally flat riding, and the large chainring for riding downhill or with a tailwind.

The cogs are used the opposite way. The largest cogs are for climbing hills or slopes or for riding against a headwind, and the smallest cogs are for descending hills or for riding on the flat with a tailwind.

If you have not already done so, make a grid chart for the gearing on your bicycle as described in Chapter 3. A grid chart shows exactly where your gears are located. And by glancing down at the drive train, you can immediately identify which development you are in.

On most bikes 70 percent of your pedaling can be done without shifting from the middle chainring. You need shift chainrings only if you require a development higher or lower than is available on the middle chainring.

You'll notice that the steps (difference in number of teeth) between the cogs is smaller than between the chainrings. Thus in selecting which gear to use, you choose the chainring first. You can then make smaller adjustments by changing cogs.

For uphill riding select the small chainring and a large cog. For a very steep hill, shift to the largest cog. For level riding select the middle chainring and a medium-sized cog. For descending a slope, or riding with the wind at your back, select the largest chainring and a smaller cog.

To become adept at shifting gears, start off in the middle chainring and practice moving the rear derailleur onto each of the cogs in turn. After you acquire dexterity with the right lever, then practice shifting chainrings with the left lever. Finally, practice some double shifts.

Derailleur Gears Run Silently

Once shifted onto the selected cog and chainring, derailleur gears should run silently. However, with friction shifting, a rattling sound indicates that the right gearshift lever needs a slight adjustment. With a properly adjusted indexed shifting system, the cogs should always run noiselessly.

A scraping sound indicates that the chain is rubbing against the front derailleur cage. A small adjustment to the left lever will restore silence. Moving from a smaller to a larger cog, or vice versa, may cause enough chain deflection to require an adjustment to the left lever.

Since derailleur gears cannot be shifted once the bike has stopped, always shift down into a larger cog before you stop riding. You will then be able to start off again in a comfortably low gear.

Conquer Hills with Good Technique

Most novices regard hill climbing as their biggest obstacle. True, it does take a little more effort, energy, and stamina to pedal uphill. But what counts most is good technique. If you keep your pedals spinning briskly in low gears, you will not only learn to conquer hills. You will actively seek out rides with the longest, most challenging hills, for you have to ride up hills to enjoy the most dramatic scenery.

All the most scenic tours traverse hills. Thus to go on an extended tour you must be able to climb hills, any reasonable hill, that is, without walking. There's no scenery, fun, or challenge in riding on the flatlands.

The secret of climbing hills is to select a low gear that is comfortable and provides a rhythm that you can stay with indefinitely without getting out of breath or fatigued. On a long, steep hill you will probably have to use your lowest development and your cadence may temporarily drop below 60 r.p.m. But don't be ashamed to use a "granny" gear. You will probably pass others with higher gears who are walking.

If you have to shift down to a 21″ or 19″ development, you may think you could get off and walk uphill almost as fast. But pedaling is more efficient and besides, you're cycling not "hikeling." To get off and walk could ruin the tremendous feeling of achievement, mastery, and success that you'll experience by pedaling all the way to the top.

So keep on pedaling up every hill you can find. Soon, you'll be able to ride up any hill of any length. And you can go anywhere without giving hills a second thought.

The secret of climbing hills is to select a low gear that is comfortable and provides a rhythm you can stay with.

Twelve Successfull Hill Riding Strategies

- 1. The main secret of climbing hills is to shift into a lower gear the instant you feel resistance on the pedals. Don't wait until you're pedaling hard up the hill.

    However, if you're traveling fast as you approach the foot of the hill, stay in high gear and use your momentum to carry you up the hill as you continue to pedal. As you go up, anticipate the climbing gear you will need to shift into.

    Now, as your momentum slows—and as soon as you feel the resistance of the hill—briefly ease up on pedal pressure and shift into a smaller chainring. Then, with the last of your momentum, shift into a larger cog.

- 2. If approaching the foot of a hill at slow speed, shift into a smaller chainring the moment you feel resistance on the pedals and just before the climb begins. And don't wait until the last second to shift into a larger cog. If you wait too long, it may be difficult to shift when the drive train is under climbing load.

• 3. While climbing a hill, it's appreciably easier to shift onto a smaller cog than onto a larger cog. So when you shift down and begin to climb, try to shift onto a cog one size larger than you estimate you will need. Then if the climb proves easier than you anticipated, you can easily shift up into a slightly higher gear by moving on to the next smallest cog. (Remember, the smaller the cog, the higher the gear.)

It's much easier to shift up to a higher gear (smaller cog) while climbing than it is to try and shift down to a lower gear (larger cog). For that reason, you should never start up a hill in a high gear in the hope of shifting to a lower gear during the climb.

• 4. Try to get a running start up all hills, especially in rolling country. As soon as you reach the crest of a hill and pedaling becomes easier, shift into a higher gear and maintain your cadence while pedaling downhill. (If you prefer, you can coast down and take a rest.) Either way, try to build up speed on the downhill leg. This will give you ample momentum to carry you halfway up the next hill as you keep pedaling. As you lose momentum, shift quickly into a lower gear and pedal your way to the top. Repeat it all at the next roller coaster descent. Be prepared to shift frequently.

• 5. It takes less energy to climb a hill when seated and spinning a lower gear than it does to stand on the pedals. As anyone who has watched bicycle races may have noticed, most racers do not go down on the drops to climb. Nor do many experienced touring riders. Instead, they place their fingers on top of the handlebar (top bar), or on the brake hoods, with their hands wide apart and elbows flexed.

This position allows you to slide back in the saddle and to pull back on your arms to boost the power of each pedal stroke. In turn, this allows you to keep the back bent at a 45° angle which brings into play the big muscles in the buttocks and lower back. Even on a mountain bike, you'll climb better by crouching over at a 45° angle.

By contrast, if you sit in a more upright position while climbing, you bring into play the slightly less powerful thigh muscles rather than the stronger muscles in the lower back and buttocks.

On a long climb, however, it is preferable to change positions so that you can stress a new set of muscles while the muscles you've just been using rest and recover.

Thus on long hills, most riders alternate positions. After riding with their hands on the top bar or brake hoods, they switch to riding crouched down on the drops, then spend a shorter period in a more upright position, and finally do a few revolutions while standing on the pedals. However, the majority of time is spent with the hands on the top bar or brake hoods.

If you're using toeclips and straps — and you should be — push down and forward from the top of the pedal stroke, then pull up and back as the pedal rises. As you become a more proficient hill climber you may be able to use slightly higher gears.

• 6. "Honking," or standing on the pedals to climb a hill, is too physically demanding for most mature riders and quickly leads to breathlessness. Even many racers prefer to sit down and spin lower gears for as long as possible before beginning to honk. However, it's OK to stand up and pedal for a short distance, or for a change of pace, or if you're on a short, steep hill and it's too late to shift.

To honk, you need to push a gear higher than you would while sitting. Place the hands on the brake lever hoods, stand up, and allow the bike to rock from side to side as you stand first on one pedal and then on the other.

• 7. To climb a steep hill on a mountain bike, sit down as much as possible and keep the saddle at optimum height. Hold the handlebar grips lightly and keep looking ahead to select a route clear of rocks or logs so that you won't be stopped. On very steep slopes your front wheel may lift off the ground. To prevent this, slide forward on the saddle and also lean forward. If the rear tire begins to slide, slide backward on the saddle. If both occur together, you must lower your center of gravity by leaning forward and sliding back in the saddle simultaneously.

• 8. When pedaling up a long hill, avoid looking for the top. Many long hills have false summits. As you reach what you think is the top, you see yet another uphill stretch ahead. Concentrate instead on reaching a tree or telephone post or other landmark about a quarter-mile ahead, or on covering 0.25 miles on your computer. Focus your attention on maintaining a correct riding style with shoulders wide apart and head held high. That way you can enjoy the scenery while you hum a tune and congratulate yourself on having done so well so far.

On a hairpin bend, or on any uphill curve, you can make the grade easier by riding as near as possible to the outside of the curve. If there is no traffic about, and none is likely, you can ride the outside of the curve, even if it means riding on the far left side of the road. But if there is any likelihood of traffic, stay in your lane while riding as closely as you can to the outside of the curve.

• **9.** Don't hesitate to take short rests. While climbing, I often rest for one minute in every 5, or for 3 minutes in every 15, or for six minutes during every half hour.

But limit rest stops while climbing to a maximum of 10 minutes. To get on again, get astride the bike, place one foot in the toeclip, and start off. Place the other foot on the underside of the pedal and generate a quick burst of speed. Use this momentum to insert your other foot in the toeclip — unnecessary, of course, with clipless pedals.

Some riders prefer to face downhill, mount the bike, push off, and position both toeclips; they then turn around and begin climbing once more.

• **10.** Stay under control when descending a long grade. Be able to stop within 40 yards. Unless you're in a race, I recommend staying at under 30 m.p.h. A deer or a dog could dash out, or you could be moving too fast to stay in your lane during a turn. Watch for rocks, loose gravel, cattle guards, obstructions, and vehicles. Try to anticipate where you'll need to brake and slow down gradually. Always slow before entering a curve. By sitting upright you can create more wind resistance to slow you down.

If you must brake on a long descent, pump the brakes alternately to prevent overheating or fading. Apply the rear brake gently for 3 seconds, then release and simultaneously apply the front brake gently for 3 seconds. Be extra careful if the road is wet. If you skid, steer into the skid and pedal to accelerate. Allow more stopping distance when it's raining.

Whenever you need more braking power, squeeze the rear brake harder. Never slam on the front brake. If you must apply the front brake hard, slide back toward the rear of the saddle. Grasp the brake levers firmly and apply pressure evenly with both hands.

•   11. On many hills you can coast or freewheel down without having to brake. To do so, shift into a higher gear and keep your hands near the brake levers. If you need more speed, you can "tuck-in" to decrease wind resistance. Slide back on the saddle and crouch down over the handlebars with hands near the brake levers, with knees and elbows drawn close in to the body, and with cranks horizontal.

•   12. Even in cold weather you can perspire while climbing a long hill. If you then face a long descent down the other side in cold weather, stop and pull on an extra sweater, windbreaker, and gloves. Otherwise you can become uncomfortably cold on the way down and you can experience hypothermia.

CHAPTER 8

How To Boost Your Energy and Stamina — and Overcome Fatigue Forever

*I*f you are often tired and easily fatigued, bicycling regularly can help you mobilize huge reserves of energy. Most beginners are astounded by how far they can pedal after a few weeks of easy riding. Any healthy person should be easily able to build amazing resources of energy and stamina by (1) eating a diet high in complex-carbohydrates, especially whole grains and tubers; and (2) by challenging the body with increasing amounts of exercise.

Challenge the body with a ride of 5 miles and it will mobilize the energy you need to ride 5 miles the next time plus providing a reserve in addition. Two days later, you'll find you can probably ride six miles without feeling tired. In two more days, you'll be able to ride 7 miles. And so on. By increasingly challenging the body with slightly larger increments of exercise, the body will respond by mobilizing the additional energy you need. In no time at all, you'll be able to ride 10 miles, then 20 miles, then 30 miles and more without feeling tired or fatigued.

Within a few months many beginning bicyclists are able to ride 50 miles a day through hilly country. The more often you ride, the more easily the miles melt away. Most adults who make the effort and really go for it seldom give up bicycling afterward.

Before beginning any exercise program, you should have your physician's approval to exercise. During your physical checkup, explain your proposed fitness program to your doctor. Assuming you are under a physician's supervision, gradually increasing increments of aerobic conditioning may still be the best way to recover from a heart attack, hypertension, or similar cardiac dysfunction. To prevent a recurrence, it's more essential than ever that you keep exercising regularly.

Overdoing It Is Out

It isn't necessary to push yourself hard to mobilize energy. Today moderation is in; overdoing it is out. The no pain-no gain ethic and the "go for the burn" principle have no place in the current fitness renaissance. Exercise physiologists have learned that we can achieve the same health benefits, and reach the same levels of fitness, without subjecting ourselves to discomfort or stress.

The only essential is that you must keep on bicycling regularly, several times a week if possible. If you're unable to bicycle on weekdays, you can still improve your fitness by swimming or brisk walking. You can then bicycle on weekends.

The important thing is never to give up on your exercise program or to miss a session. According to the Centers for Disease Control in Atlanta, only eight percent of Americans exercise enough to gain any important health benefit. The majority of those who begin an exercise program give up after a few weeks or months. Half the bicycles purchased by adults are ridden fewer than six times. The majority of others are used only for casual riding.

Regardless of your age, refuse to hang your bicycle up in the garage to gather dust. According to Dr. Fred W. Kasch, director of the Exercise Physiology Laboratory at San Diego State University, it is still possible to become physically fit even if you haven't exercised for years. In a study of men aged 45–55, Dr. Kasch found that those who had rarely exercised in the past could achieve a level of fitness almost equal to that of men who had exercised regularly for over ten years.

So don't allow any excuses. Find a convenient time slot for exercise and have your bicycle and clothes laid out the night before. Give exercise top priority. Change your lifestyle so that you exercise at every opportunity. Join the health and fitness culture. Break all ties with the couch potato way of life. Begin to see joy and pleasure in physical exertion. Study and learn all you can about bicycling. Become an expert. Subscribe to bicycling magazines and join a bicycle club.

Pedaling this touring bicycle with full camping gear, 79-year old Robert C. Hammersmith, a retired civil engineer from Rockland, California, not long ago completed his second ride across the U.S. Camping all the way, he covered 4,487 miles in 70 days.

And don't be satisfied with a bare minimum of exercise. If you pedal slowly and coast often, you won't improve your health and fitness very much.

To achieve any real benefit from cycling, or other exercise, you must exercise briskly enough to raise your heartbeat level to 70–85 percent of its safe maximum level for at least 20 minutes on 3 nonconsecutive days each week.

This can be done in one of two ways.

Aerobic Conditioning

Aerobic training conditions your heart and lungs by keeping your heartbeat in the "target zone" for a minimum of 20 minutes at each exercise session. To determine your target rate, subtract your age from 220. Assuming you are aged 40, then 220 − 40 = 180, your maximum permissible heartbeat rate. Your safe aerobic exercise target zone lies between 70 and 85 percent of 180. Multiplying 180

× 0.7 = 126, the lower limit; and multiplying 180 × 0.85 = 153, the upper limit of the target zone.

Thus at age 40 your aerobic target zone would be 126–153 beats per minute. At no time should you ever exceed your maximum heartbeat rate of 180 beats per minute.

Because women have smaller hearts and lungs, I recommend that at first women reduce their target zone range by 14 percent. This simple means multiplying the previous target zone range by 0.86. Thus for a 40-year-old-women, the previous 126–153 range becomes 108–132. However, with steady training, many women can eventually equal the performance of men.

For cardiac improvement a 40-year-old male should keep the heartbeat range between 126 and 153 beats per minute for a minimum of 20 minutes per session. Ideally, you should exercise three to four times each week on nonconsecutive days.

The target zone is intended to challenge your heart, lungs, and muscles, not to stress or harm them. To get your heart rate into the target zone you normally will have to spin the pedals in the 70–90 r.p.m. range or higher. If at any time while exercising you are unable to talk without feeling breathless, you are overdoing it.

At first you may be able to stay in the target zone for only a brief period. Don't push yourself too hard. Just keep exercising regularly. After a few sessions, the cardiovascular system will respond to aerobic conditioning so that within a month a significant improvement should occur.

How a Bicycle Computer Can Help You Train

To take your pulse, stop riding and place a finger or thumb on your wrist artery and count the number of beats in 15 seconds. Then multiply by 4. Continue the ride immediately. Stop only once during each session, preferably near the end of the ride. If your pulse is below the target zone, very gradually increase speed, distance, and duration. If it rises above the zone limits, drop to an easier pace.

Taking your pulse is easier if you have a bicycle computer. Even the most elementary computer has a digital stop watch. While riding you can feel your throat pulse with the fingers of one hand and count the number of beats during a 10-second period. Multiplying this figure by 6 gives the number of heartbeats per minute.

More advanced computers incorporate a special pulse monitor operated by a sensor worn on the chest or the earlobe. Some computers sound an alarm when you exceed or drop below your target zone. Others provide 16 hours of pulse memory, allowing you to see how hard your heart was worked during each stage of your workout.

Still other computers display your pedal cadence, and one model even includes an altimeter showing the cumulative elevation gain of all hills you have ridden up. You can even get a triathlon version for swimming, running, and bicycling. Computers that show pedal cadence can be a great help in maintaining an even rhythm within the 60–95 r.p.m. range.

Even the most elementary computer continuously shows speed, trip distance, cumulative distance, and a digital stop watch. Each function can be changed by pressing a button. With such a simple model you can still measure cadence by counting your pedal revolutions against the seconds on the stop watch.

As with all such devices, the more sophisticated and complex the computer, the more expensive it is and the more likely it is to break down. In practice, many new computers fail within the first 30 days. All are swiftly replaced by the bike shop or manufacturer. But once a computer has operated successfully during a month of rides, it usually continues to perform dependably.

You should also record your pulse rate one minute after you cease to exercise. It should have begun to drop. If it hasn't, you're probably overdoing it.

Start Out in the Comfort Zone

If staying in the target zone is uncomfortable, try staying in the "comfort zone" instead. You calculate the comfort zone by subtracting your age from 225 and multiplying by 0.6. (Example: 225 − age 40 = 185 × 0.6 = 111 beats per minute.) Few beginners have difficulty staying in the comfort zone.

As your heart and muscles become conditioned to the comfort zone, you can begin to increase the pace and allow your heart to beat faster — always, of course, without incurring discomfort.

The same effect occurs as you reach the target zone and begin to stay in it longer. Your heartbeat will steadily become slower under the same workload. It will recover more rapidly from exercise, and will drop back more swiftly to its resting pulse rate. Week by week, your resting pulse rate will steadily diminish. Then as you gradually exercise for longer periods, the capacity of your heart to handle exertion will show a significant and steady increase. Eventually, you will be able to stay in the target zone for 30 minutes or longer.

Whenever you feel like putting off bicycling because it's too windy or cold, or you don't feel like it, force yourself to get started. (This naturally exempts a bona fide health reason.) But if it's raining, go for a swim instead. Or take a brisk walk, or pedal on an indoor trainer. You'll always come back feeling refreshed and invigorated.

LSD Conditioning—Long Steady Distance

You can improve your energy, fitness, and stamina by riding either faster or farther. While aerobic conditioning emphasizes riding faster — and is preferred by people with little time — the focus of LSD conditioning is on riding farther while maintaining the same comfortable pace.

Admittedly, LSD conditioning may not produce the dramatic benefits of aerobic training. But it is easier on older riders and it very definitely will improve your fitness and keep you in top shape. Instead of riding in the target zone for 20–30 minutes, however, you may need to ride at a steady pace for two hours to achieve the same benefit.

In other words, you ride at your best speed over a longer distance while never reaching the point of exhaustion or fatigue. If you plan to take a long tour, LSD conditioning will prepare you at least as well as aerobic conditioning.

You should still take your pulse occasionally, near the end of each ride, and you should not exceed the upper limit of your aerobic target zone. But emphasis is on going the distance, not on raising the pulse rate.

Beginning to Exercise

If you have been inactive for years, it is often better to begin by walking instead of bicycling. In any event, begin very gradually and never become tired or fatigued. Too, avoid any sudden spurts. Keep increasing your walking distance until you can walk 3 miles in one hour. Not until you have attained this basic level of fitness should you begin to ride a bicycle. If you have a knee problem that prevents you from walking, either undertake a comparable swimming fitness program or ride on an indoor training bicycle.

When you begin to bicycle, set goals for time rather than for speed or distance. Start by bicycling for 20 minutes. When you're comfortable with that, increase to 25 minutes, then to 30, 40, 50, and 60 minutes. At that point change to a distance goal. Ride 10 miles, then 12, then 14, 16, 18, and 20 miles at a time. By the time you're riding 20 miles, your resting pulse rate should have dropped significantly and you should be ready for either aerobic or LSD conditioning.

Advises David B. Rusling, tour manager of Backcountry Bicycle Tours, "Adults should start out by bicycling slowly. Add miles gradually week by week as you ride. Make sure you spin using a high pedal cadence to avoid sore knees. Shift around on the bike to avoid getting sore from sitting in one position too long. The bottom line is to keep cycling fun."

Stretch, Start Slowly, and Work Up to Speed

Always stretch and warm up before exercising. Using a smooth, fluid movement, do a few stretching exercises like toe touching, swinging the torso, or yoga postures. Stretch all leg muscles thoroughly. Then spend a few minutes pedaling easily in low gears to warm up and loosen leg muscles. If you're already into aerobic conditioning, spend a few more minutes spinning the pedals as you gradually work up into your target zone.

Likewise, ease down on speed as your exercise session ends. Spend several minutes gradually reducing speed and cooling down. Then dismount and spend two minutes walking to prevent blood pooling in the legs. Finally, repeat the same stretches you did at the beginning. Avoid rushing into a hot shower or sauna immediately after you finish. Either can send blood pressure soaring.

Once you can stay in the aerobic target zone for 15–20 minutes, or have achieved a fairly competent level of LSD conditioning, you are ready to progress to interval training.

Building Endurance Through Interval Training

Designed to increase endurance while racing, interval training consists of pedaling intensely for a short period followed by pedaling through a slower recovery period. Usually the interval of intense effort lasts 15–60 seconds, followed by a recovery interval of 30–90 seconds. The intervals are then repeated until the rider has spent a total of 10–20 minutes riding at full intensity.

Racers frequently ride a series of intervals, such as 15 thirty-second intervals, each followed by a recovery interval. Or they may do 10 thirty-second intervals followed by 20 fifteen-second intervals and wind up with some longer work intervals.

Thorough warmup and cooldown periods are essential for interval training. Gears are not usually shifted during the work or recovery intervals. During the work interval, it's important to give it everything you've got and to maintain the same speed throughout the interval. If you have to slow down, you're pushing too hard.

A modified form of interval training can be used with LSD conditioning. For instance, you can ride harder for 3–5 minutes, followed by 5 minutes of recovery. Or you can alternate 3 minutes of harder pedaling with 3 minutes of easier pedaling. You might also try riding at 10 m.p.h. for 30 minutes followed by 15 m.p.h. for 15 minutes. Naturally you would not exert yourself as vigorously as when doing shorter intervals. Yet the overall effect would be to increase your endurance and strength.

How to Train for a Century (100-mile) Ride

Interval training works best if you practice it several times each week. One advantage is that, if your exercise time is limited, you can still acquire the proficiency to ride long distances. If you're training for a century, you can obtain almost as much training benefit by riding only 25 miles at a fast pace, as by going 80 miles at a moderate speed.

Most people under 50 who are reasonably fit can manage to ride a century within a year of beginning to bicycle regularly. Most centuries allow riders 10–11 hours to complete the 100-mile distance. For your first attempt use a road bike fitted with 27" × 1 ⅛", or with 700 × 25, tires and plan to ride at about 12 m.p.h.

To train for a century you can use another modified form of interval training. Set 3 different speeds for yourself: Easy is to be a relaxed pace; Century is to be 12 m.p.h.; and Brisk is to be faster.

Work out a daily riding program like the one outlined in Table 8.1.

Each week add one mile to the beginning weekday distance until you reach the maximum distance. Each Saturday add 5 miles and each Sunday add 2 miles. Exceed the maximum distance only on weekends, and then only if you feel like going farther.

You can also integrate aerobic conditioning and interval training into this program, but only on alternate days. The essential thing is to make one really long ride each week. Almost everyone who stays

Table 8.1 **Daily Riding Program**

Day of Week	Begin	Pace	Maximum
Monday	7 miles	Easy	17 miles
Tuesday	10	Century	20
Wednesday	12	Brisk	22
Thursday	R E S T D A Y		
Friday	10	Century	20
Saturday	30	Century	80
Sunday	10	Century	30

with such a program, and can ride 80 miles at 12 m.p.h., is able to complete a century. Nowadays, most century events include an optional and shorter metric century of 100 kilometers for those unable to ride 100 miles.

If a choice of terrain is available, alternate a hilly ride one day with a faster ride on a flat stretch the following day. The same training program would prepare you very adequately for any kind of extended or difficult tour.

Each of these conditioning techniques has been developed for road bikes. Yet you can use the same techniques when riding a mountain bike. Furthermore, riding up steep hills on unpaved roads or trails provides superb conditioning, as does maintaining a faster pace on level areas while using fat tires. It is often possible to ride a mountain bike in cooler weather than would be enjoyable on a road bike.

Continue to Exercise Year-Round

In some areas, like south Texas or southern California, bicycling is enjoyable all year. But in northern states it's best to place your bicycle on an indoor trainer during winter. Using aerobic or LSD conditioning, or interval training, can help to break the monotony of riding indoors.

And while bicycling does exercise most muscle groups, the legs receive the greatest workout. Thus during winter, you can alternate indoor bicycling with calisthenics, swimming, brisk walking, or cross-country skiing, which also exercise arms, trunk, and abdomen.

Whichever type of workout you choose, always maintain good riding style. Ride like a pro, using good form with pedals spinning and elbows flexed. As you do, the bicycle will become an extension of your body. You will pedal with a supple fluidity that maintains your cadence at roughly the same brisk pace over every type of condition and terrain.

You will find yourself able to ride long distances without fatigue. And you will seldom, if ever, run out of energy.

CHAPTER 9

Staying Safe on Your Bicycle

Bicycle-vehicle accidents involving bicyclists aged 25 or over are quite rare. Most adult bicyclists never have a serious accident. Unless you race, or do much off-road biking, chances are good that you won't even take a minor spill.

As an adult, then, the first thing to realize is that risk of tangling with a vehicle is extremely low. The second is that studies by the American Automobile Association, and other safety organizations, have shown that of those accidents in which adults have been involved, 70 percent could have been avoided had the bicyclist taken precautionary action.

This doesn't mean that the average bicycle-vehicle accident is the bicyclist's fault. According to the AAA *World Magazine* (March–April 1988), in a high percentage of bicycle-car accidents, the auto driver is at fault.

What it does imply is that a bicycle is far more nimble and agile than an automobile. Thus a bicyclist can react to a situation, and can take evasive action, much more swiftly than a motorist can. By learning to ride defensively, we can avoid almost all risk of an accident.

The first step towards safe riding is to check your bike over carefully before leaving home (see the checklist at the beginning of Chapter 5). Make sure that the wheels are secure and the brakes in good working order. You should replace worn tires, tubes and brake and gear cables before leaving home. It is especially important to check the mechanical condition of your bike frequently if you bought it at a discount store, where it may have been assembled by poorly trained employees.

We've all driven cars and know how difficult it is to see a small object such as a bicycle or pedestrian. Most drivers are looking only for large objects. Small objects, such as bicycles, are slow to register in the central processing system of the average driver's brain. Thus most bicycle-auto accidents occur because the motorist fails to see the bicyclist.

Bearing this in mind, here are the cardinal rules for riding safely and accident-free.

Rules of the Road for Bicyclists

Always Ride on the Right

Always stay to the right and obey all traffic rules and signs exactly as if you were driving an automobile. A bicycle is a legal vehicle in all 50 states, and you are legally obligated to keep to the right. Riding on the left confuses motorists and places you in imminent danger of a head-on collision with every vehicle you meet. One-fifth of all car-bicycle accidents occur as a result of the bicyclist riding on the left. There is no advantage whatever in facing oncoming traffic, and riding on the left can be hazardous at intersections. In the northwestern states, you may be ticketed for riding on the left.

(Naturally, if touring in countries like Britain, Ireland, Australia, or New Zealand, you do ride on the left. This takes a little getting used to at first. But I've found that once I start off on the left, I can easily remain there the rest of the day.)

Never Ride at Night

Never ride after dark, or at dusk, or in fog or heavy rain, or in poor visibility of any kind. Over 40 percent of collisions between bicycles and vehicles occur between 6 P.M. and 6 A.M., mostly in the dark. It's a good idea to carry reflective legbands or a bicycle light in case you get caught in the dark. Ankle lights are lightweight and provide additional visibility by bobbing up and down as you pedal.

Be cautious, also, when the sun is rising or setting. Even in clear weather, there is a strong possibility that a driver heading toward a low sun may not see you. Give such drivers a wide berth, and whenever you are cycling directly into the sun, monitor traffic behind you especially carefully with your rear-view mirror.

Something to remember is that two or more bicyclists riding in single file are more visible than a single rider and cause motorists to exercise greater care.

BIKECENTENNIAL PHOTO BY GARY MACFADDEN

Wearing a helmet dramatically reduces your chances of suffering serious injury in an accident. A variety of effective, lightweight helmets is now available for cyclists of all ages.

Always Wear a Helmet

Almost all fatalities resulting from bicycle accidents are caused by injuries to the head and brain. Yet statistics show that almost 80 percent of these accidents could have been entirely prevented by wearing a helmet.

Additionally, wearing a helmet, along with a bright jersey, gives you a smart, professional look and it distinguishes you from casual riders and youngsters, many of whom ride carelessly and give motorists cause for concern. Motorists recognize that bicyclists who wear helmets and bright, visible attire are responsible, law-abiding road users. As a result, most auto drivers show greater respect.

The old leather-covered hairnet helmet has long been replaced by lightweight hard-shell helmets that are far more effective. More recently, a new generation of shell-less all-foam helmets weighing only half a pound or so have become very popular. A wide selection of these attractive lightweights is now available. Made of dense Styrofoam, and without an outer shell, they depend on shock absorbency for protection and they are enclosed only by a colorful fabric cover. They are light, cool, airy, brightly visible, and very comfortable.

Most helmets have an active ventilation system that pulls air through, making it very little hotter to wear a helmet than to go bareheaded. Pads fastened with Velcro to the inside of the helmet are used to ensure a snug fit without being tight. And though the quick-release chinstrap may seem inconvenient at first, most bicyclists become completely accustomed to a helmet after a single ride.

Helmets come in different shapes, styles, and sizes. Try on several to find the one that looks and fits best. A helmet should also permit good visibility. Most important, make sure that any helmet you buy has been approved by either ANSI (American National Standards Institute) or the Snell Memorial Foundation. Both submit helmets to rigid energy-absorbing tests before approval. ANSI approval is considered sufficient for most types of riding while Snell-approved helmets must meet even higher impact-test standards. A helmet approved by one or the other must be worn at all amateur races sanctioned by the United States Cycling Federation (USCF).

Hard-shell helmets are still available. Consisting of a rigid polymer outer shell, they contain a polystyrene foam liner and they are preferred by some riders who believe they provide superior protection. However, tests have shown that soft-shell helmets provide equal protection.

Because materials used in helmets deteriorate with time, helmets should be replaced every 5 years. If you crash and suspect that your helmet may have an invisible hairline fracture, most manufacturers will check it and, if damaged, replace it free of charge.

Be Highly Visible

Whether you wear regular clothing or cyclewear, always choose the brightest colors. Bright yellow, orange, or pink are the colors most readily seen by motorists. Nowadays, sporty, fashionable designer bikewear is available in bold new colors like neon green and hot pink, and many are fluorescent for greater visibility.

Raingear should also be bright yellow or orange with reflective strips for greater visibility. Bright yellow touring bags are also available. And many soft-shell helmet covers also sport vibrant colors.

Some touring cyclists still use bright orange flags carried aloft on a plastic rod. However, if you have a brightly colored helmet, jersey, and touring bags, a flag is really unnecessary. Besides, it creates added wind resistance.

If you bicycle in ordinary clothes, a white shirt and a yellow nylon windbreaker are both easily seen from a distance.

Always Use a Rear-View Mirror

In light winds you can hear cars approaching from behind, but in stronger winds you must glance in your rear-view mirror to check on vehicles approaching from the rear. The best rear-view is provided by Third Eye plastic ball-and-socket mirrors, which have a large, round adjustable mirror on a long arm. They will fit onto either glasses or a helmet. If you wear glasses, it's a good idea to use an elastic sports strap around the back of the head to hold your glasses and mirror in place.

Mirrors are also available to fit on handlebars or brake levers, but these are easily damaged especially when you must turn the bicycle upside down for repairs or carry it inside a car. Nonetheless, some easily detachable models seem worthwhile.

Never Wear Headphones

You should never wear headphones while bicycling. You must be able to listen: first, for cars; and second, to your gears so that you can adjust them to run silently.

Never Ride Through a Tunnel

Some short tunnels in the Pacific Northwest may have pushbutton controls that warn motorists that a bicyclist is inside the tunnel. Elsewhere, don't attempt it. If there is a sidewalk wide enough to accommodate you and the bicycle, you can walk through a short tunnel provided it is lighted or you have a powerful flashlight. Otherwise, hitch a ride through on a pickup truck.

Scan Ahead for Potential Hazards

Look well ahead and try to identify possible dangers in advance. Keep at least 4 feet away from parked cars and watch for people inside, though headrests may impede your view. People may step out from between parked cars or a car door can be flung open in your face. If a car pulls to the side of the road ahead of you, be especially alert for opening doors. Watch also for vehicles entering from cross streets or driveways. Always assume they haven't seen you.

How to Stay Safe on the Highway

Highways with wide shoulders are always safer than roads without shoulders. When riding a two-lane highway without shoulders, watch for vehicles approaching from both in front and behind. For example, a car may be overtaking you while at the same time, another car may overtake it. The second driver cannot see you from the far-back point at which he began to overtake.

Or a car from behind, and a car from in front, may pass each other immediately abreast of you. In either case, if the road is narrow, the safest thing to do is to slow down, turn on to the shoulder, and stop.

The same defensive action should be used to deal with a car that is approaching from in front while another approaching car is overtaking it in your lane. The overtaking driver simply cannot see you from the far-back distance at which he began to overtake.

While such incidents are comparatively rare, you should stay alert to the possibility. Try to anticipate them in time to slow down and get off the road safely. With a mountain bike you can safely take to the shoulder without risking a spill. But on road bikes with narrow tires, it's best to slow down before turning onto the grass or dirt shoulder and stopping.

The law requires bicycles to be ridden as far to the right as practicable. Most experienced riders stay 3–4 feet from the road edge. If an overtaking car appears to be uncomfortably close, they still have 2–3 feet of space in which to move closer to the edge.

You should never deliberately block or slow down cars behind you. Wherever there is any traffic about, you must always ride in single file. If one or more cars are unable to overtake and pass you, stop and allow them to go by.

Finally, if you stop to rest or check your bike, push it completely off the road.

Watch Out for Other Hazards

Other possible hazards to watch for are rough pavement, potholes, steel manhole covers, painted pavement, bridge expansion joints, steel or wood bridge surfaces, oil patches, gravel, ice, water, wet leaves, or cinders, on any of which you can skid or slide, particularly in wet weather. Always cross railway and streetcar tracks and cattle guards at right angles. They, too, can be slippery when wet.

Sand patches, which often build up at intersections, corners, and the bottoms of hills, can be especially treacherous. Sand is particularly tricky if you are turning; the best tactic is to slow down, stop pedaling, and steer in a straight line until you're out of the sand.

Although most sewer gratings with parallel grid bars have been removed, some may still remain and these can swallow a bicycle wheel. Low-water crossings (fords) in Texas and elsewhere — where shallow water runs continuously across a roadway — can become coated with algae that is so unbelievably slippery that your bike can slide sideways under you. To cross one safely, have only sufficient momentum to reach the other side without pedaling. Don't pedal, brake, or wobble en route. If the ford is too long or too deep, hitch a ride across on a pick-up truck.

Allow for Less Efficient Braking in Wet Weather

Wet weather cuts the efficiency of bicycle brakes in half. On a wet road you need nearly 60 feet to stop at 15 m.p.h. In wet conditions you should begin to brake much sooner than normal. And to prevent skidding, you should also avoid braking hard on a wet road. If you must stop quickly, hunch down on the drops while you sit well back in the saddle and pump the brakes.

Be Doubly Careful at Intersections

Intersections are the most hazardous area for bicyclists, especially busy, multilane intersections with separate left-turn traffic lanes. To begin with, a bicycle is too small to trigger the buried coils that switch on the left-turn signal. So if you decide to go into the left-turn lane, you must allow a car to take first place.

Another situation: if you stop at the curb and plan to ride straight across, the car alongside you may plan to turn right. But you can't see his turn signals. Or if you plan to turn right and he turns right at the same time, there's going to be a squeeze.

If you must turn left at a multilane intersection, consider riding straight across to the other side, then crossing as a pedestrian. The same strategy may be advisable when turning left at any intersection. The reason is that motorists in the opposite lane may not see you.

At intersections of two-lane roads, always yield to motorists unless they signal you to go ahead. At an intersection with a traffic light, always start off promptly on the green light. Don't hold up traffic while you place your second foot in the toeclip.

Be exceptionally careful at all intersections, even those with stop signs (which cyclists, as well as motorists, should obey). When a bicyclist has the right of way at a stop sign, a car coming from the left may fail to see the bicyclist. Most accidents at intersections occur because the motorist doesn't see the bicyclist.

Too, never try to beat a red light. A motorist may try to beat it at the same time. And always yield at "yield" signs.

A bicyclist must use hand signals to indicate turns. For a left turn, extend the left arm out to the side. For a right turn, either extend the right arm or hold the left arm up with elbow bent.

Avoid Rush-Hour Traffic

Try to avoid bicycling in or near cities during busy weekday rush-hour periods. In most places traffic is busiest between 7–9 a.m. and 3:30–6 p.m. Traffic is usually light on both Saturday and Sunday mornings but builds up later in the day. Early on Sunday morning, until around 10 a.m., you can ride safely almost anywhere.

Most experienced bicyclists consider bicycle paths to be more dangerous than streets or roads. There are two types: painted paths that run along the edge of a road; and bicycle paths that are completely separate from streets.

When riding on bike paths that border roads, you must constantly watch for car doors opening or for drivers turning out of driveways. And at intersections these bike paths usually disappear, leaving the bicyclist to fend for herself or himself. (In Boulder, Colorado, and some other bike-friendly cities, bicyclists have their own left-turn lanes.)

The trouble is that separate bike paths are frequently cluttered by joggers, pedestrians, and slow bicyclists, all of whom have the right of way over fast bicyclists.

Frankly, I recommend that adult bicyclists avoid all traffic problems by using their cars to transport themselves and their bicycles out of congested urban areas and into safe, rural locales before beginning to bicycle. Even though I live in a city of only 25,000, I drive out at least 12 miles in order to reach traffic-free back roads before beginning to ride.

How to Handle Dogs

In some areas, loose dogs can be a hazard. If one dashes out at you, point back at its house and in a loud, stern voice, order it to return immediately; 50 percent of dogs will turn back.

If a dog continues on, you might consider outriding it. If this isn't practical, stop, get off, and place the bicycle between you and the dog. Continue ordering the dog back. If that doesn't work, spray the dog with water from your water bottle. As a last resort, place the bike on the ground and throw rocks at the dog.

If dogs appear to be a hazard in your area, we recommend purchasing a can of Halt, a dog repellent endorsed by the U.S. Post Office. It is sold at many bike shops. Even though it's difficult to hit a dog's head while riding, the noise and sight of the yellow jet will cause most dogs to turn back. Otherwise, get off and spray the dog in the face. It will be unable to see for several minutes.

In rural areas, vultures, deer, cattle, sheep, goats, and horses may dash out in front of a bicycle and can cause a collision.

Never Show Your Driver's License for a Bicycle Offense

Should you be stopped by a police officer and ticketed for a bicycle offense, avoid showing your driver's license as identification. If not driving a motor vehicle, you are not obligated to show a driver's license. A number of bicyclists have had bicycling violations recorded by police on their driver's licenses. If speeding on a bicycle is the offense, it can result in an increase to your auto insurance premium. Hence it's wise not to break any speed limits while bicycling.

School Buses

You must stop whenever a school bus stops, either just in front of you or approaching you from the opposite direction.

CHAPTER 10

How to Feel Terrific on
Your Bicycle

As an exercise that is virtually free of impact, bicycling causes almost no joint injuries. Thousands of athletes who have incurred orthopedic injuries in other sports have turned to bicycling as a safe way to continue to exercise, or even to compete.

Connie Carpenter, the gold medalist in the women's 1984 Olympic road race, turned to bicycling after an ankle injury prevented her from competing in the 1976 Olympic speedskating team. Another woman athlete, Danute Bankaitis-Davis, took up cycling and became a member of the 1985 National Cycling Team when knee and heel injuries stopped her from running.

Since one's full body weight is supported by the bicycle, bicycling is often recommended by orthopedists as a therapy for stress injuries incurred in other sports. Even overweight people can exercise successfully on a bicycle.

One reason is that the bicyclist's knee functions in a single plane of motion. It cannot be injured by twisting or turning. Hence bicyclists are seldom plagued by torn muscles, heel spurs, shin splints, or a torn Achilles tendon, all of which send athletes from other sports flocking to orthopedists.

Among the relatively few dysfunctions due to bicycling, the majority arise from riding an ill-fitting frame with a saddle that is too high or too low; from incorrect posture; from pedaling too slowly in gears that are too high; and from chafe and wear at friction points such as the hands, feet, and posterior.

BIKECENTENNIAL PHOTO BY GREG SIPLE

As a tour leader for Taylor University's Wandering Wheels program, Robert Davenport, shown here when aged 52, has cycled across the United States 22 times. Note that he uses flat (instead of the usual drop-style) handlebars, an option available on any road bike.

For advice on proper bicycle fit, see Chapter 4, "Ensuring a Correct Fit." Information on maintaining proper cadence, efficient posture, and correct riding position is given in Chapter 6. Meanwhile, Chapter 11 describes how correct bicyclewear can prevent aches and pains caused by pressure and chafe.

Most chafe and friction results from wearing improper clothing. Proper bicycle clothing is padded in the right places to eliminate discomfort. Hand numbness can be ended by wearing padded gloves; most foot problems disappear when you wear stiff-soled bicycling shoes; and a pair of bicycling shorts with padded crotch solves most saddle friction problems.

Common Bicycling Ailments and How to Prevent Them

Other possible discomfort due to bicycling can almost always be prevented by similar techniques. Here, then, is a brief review of the most common physiological problems connected with bicycling and how they may be solved or prevented.

Knee Problems

Chondromalacia, or worn cartilage behind the kneecap, is the most common knee complaint among bicyclists. While pedaling too slowly in high gears can worsen chondromalacia, most cases have existed for years before a person begins to bicycle. Pedaling a bicycle only serves to make a person aware that he or she has chondromalacia. Seldom is this condition actually caused by bicycling.

Other symptoms of chondromalacia are pain behind the kneecap, pain when climbing stairs, and pain on getting up after sitting for some time.

Nowadays, many cases of chondromalacia can be successfully treated by arthroscopy, an outpatient operation performed by an orthopedist. Naturally, whether or not arthroscopy may benefit any one individual case is something that only an orthopedist can decide. When arthroscopy is performed, it must usually be followed by 8 weeks of physical therapy to restore full motion to the joint and build up the quadricep muscles. In many cases, this restores the knee to a condition approaching its original pain-free state.

To prevent knee pain when bicycling, raise the saddle slightly, thus reducing stress on the patella (kneecap). However, the saddle should never be raised so high that the knee actually straightens out at the bottom of each pedal stroke. Always retain a few degrees of bend in the knee.

Before starting to ride, do some stretches, especially for the hamstring muscles. Then gradually warm up by riding in low gears and spinning at 65–85 r.p.m. or more. Maintain this, or an even faster cadence, throughout the ride by pedaling in low gears.

If your knees still hurt, you are either pushing yourself too hard, the bicycle doesn't fit, or you have chondromalacia.

If you use cleats, misalignment can cause rotation in the knee and hip joints, leading to overstretched muscles and tendons on one side of the leg together with uneven wear on the patella. Nowadays, most shoes come drilled for cleats and misalignment is less common. Nonetheless, if you have pain on the inside or outside of your knee, it could pay to have a complete session with a Fit-Kit at a bicycle shop. The Fit-Kit matches you to the bicycle, checks on cleat alignment, and eliminates most risk of knee injury.

Knee Tendinitis

Pedaling a bicycle may also uncover several varieties of knee tendinitis caused by an earlier nonbicycling injury or accident. This type of injury frequently does not show up until you begin to bicycle.

Tendinitis usually occurs as a pain above or below the kneecap and may be due not only to an injured tendon but to a damaged bursa. (A *bursa* is a fluid-filled sac that cushions a joint; it becomes swollen and inflamed when injured.) In any case, the solution is to stop bicycling and to exercise by swimming until the condition improves. If you have persistent or chronic tendinitis below the knee, you should have it checked by a sports orthopedist.

Known as quadricep or patella tendinitis, it is often due to stress to a tendon connecting the kneecap to the lower leg bone. The condition can be worsened through overusing the quadricep muscles by pedaling in high gears.

Popliteal tendinitis results from inflammation to the popliteal tendon on the outside of the knee when it rubs against a ligament. It can often be relieved by lowering the saddle half an inch or so.

"Burning" Sole

A painful or "burning" feeling in the soles of the feet is caused by pressing so hard on the pedals that the transverse arch of the foot is flattened, placing unusual pressure on bones and compressing nerves. Frequently, the cause is grinding away in high gears while wearing soft-soled shoes through which the pedal cages press.

The solution is to wear stiff-soled bicycling shoes together with toeclips and straps, and to spin in lower gears at a cadence of 65–95 r.p.m. or more.

If bicycling shoes aren't immediately obtainable, try wearing a metatarsal arch support, or use a sturdy pair of running shoes with stiff sides.

Leg Cramps

Muscle cramps in the legs are often due to depletion of salt, potassium, and magnesium. Take sports drinks containing electrolytes and add a pinch or two of salt to your food each day.

When a muscle cramp occurs, pinch the fold of skin immediately under the nose and above the mouth. Pinch it hard and hold—this is an acupressure point that usually releases a muscle cramp within half a minute. Alternatively, pull back on your toes while sitting. If you can stand, stand on your toes on a stair edge and lower your heels. This does an even better job of pulling out the toes and, at the same time, the cramped leg muscle.

Saddle Soreness

Saddle soreness is due to unfamiliar friction and pressure on posterior and crotch tissue. After a few beginning rides, you start to develop muscles that harden and banish all saddle discomfort.

A more painful type of saddle soreness can be caused by boils or sores that arise when chafe and sweat damage hair follicles. The solution is to wash the painful area with medicated soap and rub on rubbing alcohol. After airing it, rub in an oily body lotion. Or you can use Vaseline, cornstarch, or Noxema.

An almost certain way to invite saddle soreness is to ride on a wide-cushioned saddle. By comparison, saddles used by adult bicyclists are narrow with slender lines to prevent chafe. Nonetheless, should saddle discomfort persist, consider getting a different saddle specifically designed for male or female anatomy. Most women prefer a wider saddle with a shorter nose. Alternatively, you might experiment by changing the angle of your present saddle. Try setting the saddle level, or tilting the nose down slightly.

Yet the most successful way to prevent saddle chafe is to wear proper bicycling shorts with a padded crotch together with seamless underwear. Obviously, you should never wear jeans, cut-offs, or any other garment with a thick seam in the crotch. Many bicyclists also use talcum powder to keep the skin dry. Others use cold cream or Noxema as a lubricant.

Crotch Numbness

Crotch numbness in males is caused by compression of the pudendal nerve as it traverses the perineum. A sharp pain occurs on urinating but disappears within a few minutes. The solution is to wear bicycle shorts with a padded crotch. Standing periodically while pedaling also helps to solve this problem. If numbness still persists, adjust the saddle's angle of tilt. Otherwise, try a padded gel saddle.

In women, numbness occurs due to bending forward while riding on a road bike. This position compresses the genitals between the saddle nose and the pelvic bone. Numbness is less common in the more upright position used when riding a mountain bike. The solution is the same as that described for men. If you decide to change saddles, ask for a special woman's saddle equipped with pads to prevent genital compression.

Very rarely, riding long distances on a hard saddle can irritate critical nerves and arteries, causing temporary impotence in males.

Difficulty in achieving an erection may persist for 1 or 2 days at a time, accompanied by numbness in the crotch and buttocks regions. This dysfunction can usually be avoided by wearing padded shorts, switching to a gel-padded saddle, and standing up in the saddle at fairly frequent intervals while riding. Should symptoms persist, medical treatment is available for this condition.

Soreness in Neck and Upper Arms

Stiffness and ache in neck and shoulders can be relieved by frequently changing the position of the hands on the handlebar. The great advantage of a drop-type handlebar lies in its ability to prevent neck, shoulder, and upper arm discomfort through providing three different hand positions with accompanying changes in the angle of the back.

Should neck and shoulder soreness persist, try raising the height of the handlebars, using a stem with a shorter extension, and sliding the saddle closer to the handlebars.

You should also very adequately stretch the neck, shoulders, and arms before and after riding. While riding, relax and lower the shoulders and keep the elbows bent.

Hand Numbness

Most common among racers, hand numbness is due to gripping the handlebars tightly and keeping the palms on the handlebars for extended periods. The numbness can persist after ceasing to ride.

The solution is to wear well-padded cycling gloves. If that isn't enough, add slide-on foam handlebar grips. Keep changing hand positions on the handlebars and flutter the fingers frequently. Above all, hold the handlebar lightly, like a jockey riding a racehorse.

Overexposure to the Sun

Skin cancer is the most common form of cancer, and riders over 40, or light-skinned bicyclists of any age, should take precautions to avoid direct exposure to the intense summer sun. Particularly between 10:30 a.m. and 2:30 p.m., I always wear long sleeves and use a #15 sunscreen block on thighs, knees, legs, and the backs of hands, wrists, and neck.

If you're at all bothered by the glare of the sun, either wear prescription sunglasses or buy a pair of wraparound sports sunglasses. A gray or green tint provides the best protection. Lenses are also available that block out completely ultraviolet light, believed by some authorities to increase risk of cataracts.

For ease in fitting a rear-view mirror, try to get a plastic frame with wide earpieces. Eyeglasses will also protect your eyes from insects.

How to End a Ride

Prolonged and intense bicycling can also worsen varicose veins that may already exist on the legs. This risk can be minimized by walking for a few minutes at the end of a ride. Later, at the end of the day, rest with the legs elevated above the heart level.

Whether or not you have varicose veins, you should avoid stopping suddenly after a long ride. Doing so causes blood to pool in the legs. This condition can be easily avoided by walking for a few minutes at the end of a ride. Follow with a few backward and forward stretches, including touching the toes and raising up and down on the toes.

CHAPTER 11

Bicyclewear that Combines Comfort with Fashion and Function

Wearing improper clothing like tennis shorts, running shoes, and T-shirts to bicycle in can cause a variety of aches and pains ranging from saddle chafe to numb hands, overheating, hypothermia, and foot discomfort.

Although most beginners start out wearing makeshift clothing, the sooner you can invest in proper bikewear, the better. Proper bikewear not only prevents most saddle soreness but also prevents numb hands, helps regulate body temperature, and eliminates such foot problems as burning soles.

Made of breathable fibers that fit like a second skin, bicycle pants and jerseys wick perspiration away from the body while the fabric stays dry. Manmade synthetics have replaced almost all natural fibers in bikewear, and so many are used that you almost need a chemistry degree to evaluate them. And new-generation fibers are constantly appearing. For example, 4-channeled fibers currently being used have 20 percent more surface fiber for evaporating perspiration than such traditional favorites as polyesters and polypropylene.

Anatomically designed with a sporty, high-profile look, modern bikewear can really enhance your bicycling performance. While brand name apparel with designer colors and fabrics can be fairly expensive, several mailorder firms offer well-made house-brand shorts, jerseys, shoes, gloves, and other bikewear at prices that almost any beginner can afford.

Loose-fitting clothing that billows out in the wind can cut your cycling speed by as much as 10 percent. Thus, to minimize wind resistance, all bikewear fits snugly without being tight, something designers have accomplished by using body-hugging materials like Lycra and nylon. Cold-weather tights and jerseys are made of hollow-core fabrics that provide warmth without bulk, while a variety of raingear will keep you dry in the heaviest of rain.

You can probably economize on bikewear if you take only day rides. But for extended touring you should be prepared for changeable weather. During a single day's ride in Vermont, I started out wearing a windbreaker, sweater, gloves, and winter tights; sunbathed in shorts at midday; and then had to don raingear for the final hour.

Proper Bicyclewear Keeps You Comfortable in All Weather

Light, cool cotton-Lycra blends are used for hot weather clothing as well as several proprietary synthetic materials like X-Bio, Coolmax, or Fieldsensor that actively dispense perspiration, leaving you cool and dry. Don't forget, also, that headwinds cool you as you ride. Even on a calm day a bicyclist creates a cooling breeze of 12 m.p.h. or more simply by moving. Bicycling is invariably cooler than hiking. Nonetheless, a sweatband is helpful plus a tennis visor to wear under your helmet.

You can continue to ride in surprisingly cold weather — as low as 10°F — by using the layer method of dressing. The first layer consists of breathable underwear; the second is thermal wear, such as a jersey and sweater, to insulate you from the cold; and the third layer consists of outerwear to keep out rain, cold, and wind. Like a crosscountry skier, you can add or subtract a layer so that you stay warm without excessive perspiration. To make this work, you must have a bicycle bag in which to place the garments you remove.

A windbreaker, sweater, warm jersey, warm gloves, and nylon booties to cover your feet are almost essential for winter riding. They are also necessary for riding above timberline in Colorado, even in August.

With the appropriate clothing you can keep riding comfortably in all weathers. Here is a brief review of the principal items of bikewear.

All bikewear should be highly visible, a topic already covered along with helmets in Chapter 8.

Bicycling Shorts

Made of soft-stretching fabrics like nylon, Lycra, or cotton, bicycling shorts have long legs that protect the thighs from sun and chafe, plus a crotch that is padded with either ultrasuede chamois, or with a combination of polypropylene fleece and polyurethane foam. Both have a soft, natural feel and effectively cushion the crotch from friction. But the synthetic crotch pads have the advantage that they can be machine washed and dried.

Bike shorts are cut high in the back for extra warmth, have a reinforced outer seat, and are fastened by a drawstring or elastic waist. The best contoured shorts are made of 8 separate panels, though pairs made of 4 panels are quite adequate and less expensive. Seamless underwear is usually worn under cycling shorts. Shorts should be washed and cleaned often, especially in warm weather.

BIKECENTENNIAL PHOTO

Jim and Linda Richardson were the first cyclists to ride the complete 4,250-mile Trans-America Trail. Although helmet designs have changed since they made their ride, their comfortable, sporty bikewear is representative of that worn by today's bicycle tourists.

Special women's shorts are available with slightly shorter legs and curved hips, a higher waist, and a detachable crotch pad of foam or gel. Gel is said to distribute pressure over a larger area and to eliminate pressure points.

A new type of baggie shorts with padded crotch liner has become popular with mountain bike and touring riders. They can be worn both on and off the bike, but naturally, they create extra wind resistance.

Jerseys

The best wicking jerseys are of Lycra, cotton, polyester, or polypropylene or, perhaps by now, of some entirely new material. They are cut long and slender to hug the hips and have a large triple-section pocket in back. Both short- and long-sleeved jerseys are made, though long-sleeved ones are harder to find. For really cold weather riding, wool jerseys are still popular.

Nowadays, jerseys for hot weather are often made of mesh combined with cotton-poly knit for maximum ventilation.

Gloves

Designed to protect the hands from road shock and numbness, cycling gloves are cut off above the knuckles and have extra thick padding behind the supple leather palms, with open netting on the back for ventilation. Gloves distribute handlebar pressure evenly across the palms, preventing both vibration and chafe as well as nerve-compression numbness. They are closed by a Velcro wrist band.

You can smooth out road bumps still more by padding the handlebars with slide-on foam grips.

In cold weather, cycling gloves must be replaced with warm nylon shell mittens, or a similar cold weather glove.

Shoes

Bicycling shoes are built narrow with a toe that fits into a toeclip, and with a sole that is thin but reinforced and rigid to prevent flexing. Most shoes also have some form of cleat designed to lock the foot to the pedal and to prevent the foot from pivoting. Shoes like these enable the rider to deliver more leg power to the road and to minimize strain on the soles of the feet (often described as burning soles). Most medium-priced shoes have ventilated nylon mesh uppers. Such shoes are made primarily for use with racing and sports bicycles. They are lighter than running shoes and fairly expensive.

Touring shoes have similar qualities but look and feel more like jogging shoes. They are made with an internal plastic or metal sole stiffener ar 1 have reinforced nylon mesh uppers. Though it is stiff, the sole is also flexible enough for walking.

Most touring shoes have a built-in groove on the sole that meshes with the pedals. Other models have recessed plastic cleats with which you can walk fairly well. Incidentally, rubber protectors are available that cover all cleats, allowing you to walk without damaging the cleats.

In practice, half of all touring bicyclists ride long daily distances with neither cleats nor grooves and without tightening toeclip straps. Nonetheless, they invariably do wear special bicycle touring shoes, which can also be used for walking.

Also available are special mountain bike shoes with a rigid nylon-Fiberglas midsole. You can also ride in lightweight cycling boots, which can be used for scaling the summit of a peak after you have climbed as far as you can go by mountain bicycle. Most bicycle shoes are made in all sizes up to size 13.

Winter Training Tights

These are long-legged tights made of stretch-breathable materials that fit snugly in the riding position. Made of nylon and Lycra, with stirrups to keep the ankles from riding up, they keep you warm in cold weather without trapping moisture. Some contain knee inserts to help warm the knees. Winter training tights are not just for winter, but any time the temperature is below 60°F.

Better than the bulky wool leg warmers one still sees in use are warmup pants of polyester and acrylic that are both warm and water resistant. They can be removed when the weather warms up.

Booties

Booties are waterproof covers that fit over shoes up to the ankles, providing protection against rain and cold. An aperture in the sole accommodates most cleats. Booties are available in either Gore-tex or in less expensive nylon or neoprene. Booties are *essential* for staying comfortable in rain or cold.

Raingear

Raingear may not be worthwhile in hot weather, and in many parts of the United States it often doesn't rain for months. Thus

Plastic fenders and good quality raingear keep father and child dry while riding in the rain. Raingear and mudguards are essential equipment for touring in such rainy areas as the northeastern U.S., Europe, or New Zealand.

many western bicyclists overlook the risk of rain when planning vacation tours in the Northeast or in Europe or New Zealand.

A light, inexpensive nylon-coated shell or rainsuit is OK for day rides. But whenever there's any chance of steady rain, I'd never go on an extended tour without the best quality raingear I can afford. Hypothermia can occur in wet and windy weather in temperatures as high as 60°F.

Undoubtedly the best raingear material is Gore-tex, a fabric laminated between two layers of nylon. Gore-tex keeps out both wind and water while allowing perspiration to pass out. The only problem with this wonderfully durable, soft, and smooth fabric is its relatively high cost.

The other material is coated nylon, which is waterproof but doesn't breathe, causing perspiration to condense inside. (Water resistant, breathable versions are available but they are not waterproof.)

Matching jackets and pants of either material are available.

Jackets have sewn-in hoods that accommodate a helmet, plus a baffle-flap enclosure to prevent rain from entering the zipper.

Any coated-nylon rainsuit should have very adequate zippered vents; otherwise you will perspire heavily. Although back vents are most common, underarm vents are more effective. Pants should also have vents. Gore-tex rainsuits also have these vents.

If you ride in shorts, you may not need long-legged raingear. But in really cold, rainy weather, shorts are too cold and you'll need full-length rain pants. They should fit snugly yet be long enough to cover the ankles when the knee is bent. The cuffs should have zippers so that you can pull them on over shoes, and they should not catch on the chainrings.

For riding with shorts, rain shells are popular. These are close-fronted jackets similar to a windbreaker with a neck zipper and a large front pocket. Made of nylon with a water-repellent front and a fleece-lined back, they extend down only to the waist. They are generally suited only for warm-weather wear.

Before buying, try on a rainsuit while sitting on your bike. The pants must be long enough to cover the ankle when the knee is bent. Raingear should be bright yellow, pink, or orange with reflective strips for greater visibility.

Still available in England, if you happen to be touring there, are bright yellow plastic capes and leg chaps. Though maligned because they present a greater area to a strong crosswind, the cape-chap combination is still the only inexpensive raingear that provides *full* ventilation and allows you to stay *completely* dry. The cape covers the entire bicycle including the handlebar bag and is kept in place by two loops hooked over the thumbs. The back is tucked under you as you sit in the saddle.

To be completely effective, the cape-chaps combination must be used with mudguards; otherwise a stream of water and dirt from the tires will spray up under the cape.

Though certainly not ideal, a cape-chaps combination is still preferred by some traditionalists. The cape can be whipped on and off in seconds, making it particularly suitable for use in frequent short showers.

With any type of raingear, your bike and your touring bags will be sprayed with rain and dirt from the tires unless you have mudguards. Thus I strongly recommend lightweight plastic mudguards. Usually, only touring or mountain bikes have sufficient clearance for mudguards to fit.

Windbreakers

A lightweight nylon windbreaker is essential in cold windy weather. If you don't mind a rather loose fit, you can buy an inexpensive red or yellow zippered nylon windbreaker at a discount house or department store.

Combining form and function, and full of performance features, modern bikewear smooths out rough roads and keeps you comfortable in all seasons.

CHAPTER 12

Let Day Rides Get You into Gear

A day ride is a ride limited to a maximum of one day. It can range from 10 to 100 miles and can last from 2 to 10 hours or more. Some of the most beautiful regions of America, Europe, and other countries can be explored on one-day rides. In fact, an entire vacation can be spent star-touring, that is, staying at a central motel, hotel, or campground and, each day, taking a day ride out and back in a different direction.

Nonetheless, most day rides are devoted to fitness rather than to vacation touring. And today's fast-paced lifestyle places such demands on people's time that, even in bicycling, the trend is toward short, fast day rides that provide an intense workout. Most working people cannot devote a full day each week to taking a long ride.

For this same reason, more than half the clientele on most extended tours consists of people in their 50s, or those who are retired, and who have the leisure and money to go on rides lasting from a week to a month or more.

A local bicycle club is the best source for day rides in your area. By pooling the road knowledge of many members, clubs can offer a variety of well-tested day rides via the quietest and most scenic routes. Additionally, most clubs hold a sociable monthly meeting where you can meet other bicyclists and watch films or slides of local bicycling events. Bicycle clubs also sponsor time trials, local races, overnight or longer tours, and an annual century ride. They also offer workshops in bicycle maintenance and repair and in efficient riding skills. You can learn a tremendous amount in a short time by watching and learning from other riders.

Another excellent source of day rides for your area (or others, if you want to go farther afield) is the numerous books of bike rides which have been written for many states and regions. The best listing of these books is found in the annual *Bicycle USA Almanac* published by the League of American Wheelmen and in Bikecentennial's *Cyclosource* (see Appendix B for addresses).

Day Riding with a Bicycle Club

Undoubtedly, joining a club is the fastest way to learn where the best routes for day rides are in your region. But the actual day rides offered by clubs vary. If your club specializes in short, fast rides for busy young people, you may start out with an elite group of youthful riders, all superbly mounted on high-performance racing bikes. Within a few minutes they will have disappeared into the wild blue yonder, traveling in a pack at 30 m.p.h., and that's probably the last you will see of them on this ride. Having a rides program devoted exclusively to fast, short rides is responsible for the widely held belief that bicycle clubs are only for elite, superfast riders.

Other clubs, particularly larger ones, will offer a more varied program that includes both moderately paced rides and rides for beginners. If your club has no such program, you can make many new bicycling friends by offering to lead such rides yourself.

Local AYH (American Youth Hostels) groups also usually offer a series of day rides that are touring rather than racing oriented.

On a typical club day ride, everyone starts out together and rides at his or her own pace, following a map provided by the leader. After about two hours, you stop for refreshments at a café. Or you may be asked to bring a snack lunch. Later, you return by a different route, or perhaps by the way you came.

Almost all clubs allow guests so that newcomers can try out a ride before joining. Local day rides usually have no vehicle support. So unless it's a beginner's ride, make sure you can go the distance and maintain a respectable speed of 10–12 m.p.h. You're also expected to be self-sufficient and to be able to at least handle a flat on your own. Where appropriate, you should also carry water, adequate clothing, and raingear. Never depend on another club member to bail you out.

Tips on Group Riding

During a day ride you may want to ride in a pack with the other riders to lessen resistance against a headwind. Advice on riding in a pack is given in Chapters 7 and 15. When riding in a group of any kind, the front rider usually warns those behind of glass, potholes or other hazards by calling out, "Glass!" "Pothole!" "Stopping!" or "Car!" The lead rider also makes hand signals to indicate any turn.

Should you pass or overtake another bicyclist, always do so on her or his left, calling out, "Passing on your left!" Avoid overtaking on the right. And except in a race, never draft another rider without asking permission. Unless he or she knows you are there, the lead rider can make an abrupt turn or stop suddenly. Incidentally, to draft means to ride very closely behind one or more other riders so that they shelter you from having to pedal against a headwind.

Maps to Take You Roaming in the United States

To locate routes for day rides on your own, you must first have detailed local road maps. Half-inch-to-the-mile maps are available for virtually every county in every state. While they show no contours and few topographic details, they do show every publicly maintained road, both paved and unpaved. To order these maps you must first write for a county index to the state highway department at the state capital. You can then order individual maps. Prices are usually nominal.

More expensive but superior are topographical maps of the United States, published by the U.S. Geological Survey. They are available in these series: 7½ minutes (1:24,000 or 1″ = 2,000′) quads of approximately 6 × 8 mile sections; 15 minute (1:62,000 or 1″ = 1 mile) series, which covers 12 × 17 mile sections; and the 1:250,000 (1″ = 4 miles) series, which covers 70 × 110 mile sectors. The 7½-minute series is most practical for mountain biking; the 15-minute series for road bike day rides; and the 1:250,000 series for longer tours.

Topographical maps accurately represent all natural and man-made features and show contours, elevations, rivers, peaks, valleys, roads, and towns. With their aid you can tell whether a road is level or hilly. Roads paralleling rivers or railroads are often least hilly. To order topographical maps you must first write for an index to the state you are interested in. State indexes are obtainable from the addresses in the Appendix to this book. With the aid of such maps you can pick what seem the quietest and most scenic roads in your area. Frequently roads that do not connect two towns carry less traffic, as do older roads from which traffic has been siphoned off by a new Interstate or freeway.

Roads with wide, paved shoulders, similar to those on Interstates, frequently offer the safest riding, even though such roads may carry more traffic. You may also ride on Interstates in some Northwestern states and in Colorado, where no alternative route exists.

Use Your Car to Get Out of Town

Once you've located some potential routes on your map, drive out and reconnoiter them in your car. Look for potential problems such as narrow roads carrying trucks and RVs, congested areas, and traffic from quarries or plants.

Don't overlook the possibility that, while your city or town may be surrounded by busy roads and highways, a drive of 15–20 minutes can take you and your bike by car to the starting point of one or more quiet roads, ideal for bicycling. Many younger riders are willing to brave traffic while riding in or out of town. I don't see this as a necessity for any adult who owns a car. Provided you can park safely, it's far better to drive out through busy, congested suburbs and begin to bicycle once you're out in the country.

Again, all too many bicyclists persist in believing that day rides *must* follow a circular route that brings you back on a different road. To accomplish this you are often routed one way on a narrow, congested road with steady traffic. In reality it is often far more comfortable to go out and back on the same quiet, traffic-free road and to forget about a circular route. Coming back provides an entirely fresh view of the scenery. I certainly wouldn't ride on a busy, narrow road just to return by a different route. Yet all too many people who organize rides seem totally insensitive to traffic.

Day rides described in some, though certainly not all, books of bicycle rides suffer from this same rigid thinking. Too often, they begin and end at an urban center and then apologize for the congested roads the rider must use. How much more enjoyable these rides would be if the writers broke out of their mindset that all day rides must begin and end in a town or city.

Endless panoramas of huge Lake Taupo reward the touring cyclist on New Zealand's North Island.

Incidentally, if you contemplate moving upon retirement, it could pay to relocate in an area that offers top-rung day rides and touring throughout the year. Two such towns are Fredericksburg and Kerrville in the Hill Country of south central Texas. Even then you will want to drive a dozen miles out of Kerrville before beginning to ride. It's the country for a hundred miles or more around these towns that offers good bicycling, not the towns themselves.

To carry your bike or bikes, you may need a cartop rack. A variety of models are available, from cartop carriers carrying bikes upright on the roof to others that carry bikes on the rear of the trunk, and still others that fit inside the back of a pickup truck.

Star Touring by Day Rides

In contrast to taking a continuous tour, where each night is spent at a different place, you might consider a star-touring vacation. This implies making your base for several nights at the same motel, hotel, or campground. Each day you then bicycle out in a different direction, returning to your base for the night. After sampling all the day rides available from one base, you bicycle or drive to the next base and begin star touring from there.

Having your car along is an advantage, particularly if the distance between base towns is far. You can also use your car to drive out as far as 50 miles from your base before beginning a day ride. In this way you can cover a vastly greater variety of day rides from a single base. In some areas it is quite possible to spend two whole weeks at the same base, sampling a new ride each day with the aid of your car.

You can star tour in other countries as well as in the United States. Because of weekend tourists, always have a confirmed reservation for Saturday nights and national holidays.

The Best U.S. Towns for Star Touring

For starters, I'd suggest joining Bikecentennial, the national bicycle route information service (address in Appendix) and requesting a copy of their *Cyclosource* catalog. Listed in its pages are dozens of bicycling guidebooks that describe day rides galore. Bikecentennial's *The Cyclist's Yellow Pages,* also free to members, and the annual *Bicycle USA Almanac* issued by the League of American Wheelmen are two other treasure troves of leads and publications to top day ride locales, both in the United States and abroad. You should also write for the book catalogs of The Countryman Press and Globe Pequot Press (addresses in Appendix B), which list guidebooks to day tours in the New England and mid-Atlantic states. Through these and similar sources, you can learn about remote backroads known only to bicyclists and a few cognoscenti.

Among states or regions thereof covered by day ride guides are Arizona, California, Colorado, Connecticut, Delaware, Maine, Maryland, Massachusetts, Montana, New Hampshire, New Jersey, New York, North Carolina, Pennsylvania, Ohio, Oregon, Rhode Island, Texas, Utah, Vermont, Virginia, Washington, and Wyoming. Also included in Bikecentennial's *Cyclosource* are guides to mountain-bike day rides in these same states plus others in South Dakota, North Dakota, Idaho, and the Canadian Rockies.

I'd be rather careful about day rides on paved roads in national parks. Many of these roads are quite narrow and during the season are clogged with RVs, most of which are fitted with huge extension mirrors. By contrast, unpaved park roads frequently offer terrific mountain biking.

BIKECENTENNIAL PHOTO BY MICHAEL MCCOY

Wyoming's Yellowstone National Park offers outstanding day rides for mountain bikers.

Mountain Bicycle Day Rides

Mountain bikes can be ridden on any publicly maintained unpaved road, plus all unpaved roads on city, county, state, or federal property where vehicular traffic is allowed. All roads in national forests, even those closed to motor vehicles, are usually open to mountain bikes.

In national parks mountain bikes are permitted on all 4-wheel drive trails, or on any primitive dirt road open to vehicles. Throughout the West, bikes are free to roam vehicular tracks on all Bureau of Land Management lands — that is, huge tracts of unwooded public lands. Many Nordic ski areas also offer good mountain bike riding in summer. You'll also find many scenic trails in state forests where mountain bikes are allowed while some large state parks have networks of suitable roads.

(You should, however, ride only on walking and hiking trails where bicycles are clearly permitted and welcome. Riding on narrow trails elsewhere can interfere with hikers and give bicyclists a poor image in the eyes of fellow outdoorspeople. Moreover, bicycling on unauthorized trails on state or federal lands can earn you a ranger citation and a stiff fine. In general, there are more trails where mountain bicycles are permitted in the West than in the East.

Bicycles tend to be prohibited or unwelcome on major trail systems in the East, such as the Appalachian Trail and hiking trails in the Adirondacks and White Mountain National Forest. Naturally, you should also be careful not to ride on private roads or land without the owner's permission.)

Among the best state parks for mountain-bike day rides is Anza Borrego State Park in southern California — a desert park at its best in winter. Other good star-touring centers, or areas, for mountain bike day rides include these:

Colorado: Breckenridge, Boulder, Crested Butte, Frisco, Steamboat Springs, Vail, Winter Park.

Idaho: Ketchum; Sawtooth Mountains; and the Sawtooth National Recreation Area.

Montana: Missoula, and in most national forests, especially the Absaroka, Beartooth, Gallatin, and Snowy Mountains.

New Mexico: Gila National Forest, north of Silver City, plus national monuments like Dinosaur.

Oregon: Hood River and Rogue River National Forests.

Utah: Moab and Canyonlands National Park; also in most national forests.

Wyoming: Yellowstone National Park; Jackson Hole; along the Madison River; in most national forests; and Cody, Cooke City, Ennis, Emigrant, Nevada City and Roosevelt.

Not open to mountain biking are most narrow hiking trails, while all wilderness areas are closed to all-terrain bikes. Nonetheless, some hiking trails in western national forests have been opened to bicycling. On these authorized trails, ATB fans are welcome to enjoy the bone-rattling excitement of bombing down steep trails strewn with rocks, tree roots, marshes and other technical challenges.

Most adults, however, prefer the smoother riding available on the hundreds of old railroad beds and logging and mining roads that web the Rockies and other mountain ranges.

Incidentally, whenever you meet hikers or horse riders while mountain biking, slow down and let them by. Likewise, when overtaking them, slow down and let them know you are there. Never try to race past. If you meet a motorcycle group, it's best to pull off the road and wait until they've all gone by.

Day Rides at Bicycle Rallies, Conventions and Festivals

Bicycle rallies, conventions, festivals and other gatherings of bicyclists feature at least one day ride during each day of the event. At larger events, some of which draw thousands of bicyclists, three or more different day rides are programmed daily: a shorter ride of 25 miles; a medium distance ride of 40–50 miles; and a longer ride. At these events you'll find hundreds of participants to share workshops, rides, and camaraderie.

The best nationwide source for bicycle events (including century rides) is the publication *Bicycle USA*, free when you join the League of American Wheelmen (the national organization of bicyclists), the address for which is in the Appendix. Local bike-club newsletters also feature most events in their own and nearby states.

Centuries—The Longest Day Rides

Nowadays, most century events offer not only the standard 100-mile day ride but also shorter rides of 25 and 50 miles plus others of 25, 50, and 100 kilometers (15, 30, and 60 miles). Thus virtually any century event held within convenient driving distance offers an opportunity for a grand day ride along with a large turnout of fellow bicyclists.

Century rides are noncompetitive 100-mile or 100-kilometer fun rides. Most begin at 7 A.M. — though you can start as late as 8 A.M. — and you are given 10–12 hours to complete the 100-mile itinerary. Each participant rides at her or his own pace and there are usually three or four rest stops with food and water available. Sag wagons patrol the route and bring in sagging riders or those with mechanical problems.

Friendly, unofficial races often take place during centuries but the majority of riders are just out to enjoy the ride and to prove to themselves that they can ride 100 miles in a day. For elite ironmen some clubs offer double or even triple centuries (covering 300 miles in 24 hours). Most centuries are held in the fall.

While dozens of tandem couples participate in these bicycling events, each year sees an increasing number of day ride events and tours for tandems only. A complete list is published in the newsletter of the Tandem Club of America, the address for which is in the Appendix.

A *Little Help from the Wind*

For unscheduled day rides always try to plan a ride that takes you into the wind on the way out, and that provides a tailwind on the way back. Or you might be able to ride out through a wooded area that shields you from a headwind, and return by a more open route on which a tailwind can help speed your return. Any strategy that ensures a tailwind on the second half of the ride makes the ride easier and more enjoyable. A strong tailwind can easily help you to pedal at 20–30 m.p.h. or more.

During summer it's also good strategy to schedule a day ride as early in the day as possible. Not only do you miss the late afternoon heat and possible thunderstorms but in high mountain areas you avoid being on high ridges and high passes where afternoon lightning can occur.

CHAPTER 13

Independent Touring – the Ultimate Bicycling Experience

The air was still crisp as I wheeled my bicycle out of the guest house overlooking Loch Ness in the Scottish Highlands. I hooked on the pannier and handlebar bags and pedaled down the highway toward the Isle of Skye – 75 miles away and my destination for the day.

The road soon left the hill-girded loch and began a steady 20-mile climb through deep glens and crags to the brooding heights of Loch Cluanie. From its gaunt shores I coasted for miles down the heather-clad slopes of Glen Shiels. Then, between rows of purple mountains, I soared on downhill in a breathtaking descent that turned the roadsides into blurred ribbons of russet and green. Soon I was at sea level, riding along the hilly shores of Loch Duich.

Wide panoramas of islands, beaches, rocks, and occasional castles flowed by. Gliding on silent wheels above the great sea lochs was as exhilarating as flying. As I lunched on a rock beside Loch Alsh, I watched two gray seals cavort while a pair of buzzards cruised overhead.

At the white waterside town of Kyle I rode straight aboard the ferry while a long line of cars was left behind to await the next sailing. An hour later I rode ashore on Skye and kept right on pedaling. Trim white cottages dotted the island's treeless moors, and every second one bore a "Bed & Breakfast" sign. As the afternoon sun splashed the distant Cuillin Hills with golden light, I pulled up outside the Hilton Guest House in Broadford Village.

Minutes later, I unpacked in a comfortable bedroom with a wild seascape framed in the window. And soon I was indulging in a long relaxing soak in a hot tub bath.

The Lure of the Open Road

As a sample of solo, independent bicycle touring in Europe, this might be considered a fairly typical day. It was, in fact, the second day of a 5-week long tour that recently took me from Inverness through the Scottish Highlands, around the coasts of Ulster and Ireland, and by car ferry to France for a final ten days of cycling along the rocky shores of Brittany.

Throughout, I stayed at comfortable guest houses and small hotels, thoroughly exploding the popular misconception that exercise and comfort are incompatible. Yet most Americans continue to equate bicycle touring with strenuously puffing against headwinds and up hills, at the mercy of heat and rain, while roughing it in tents or hostels. Had I wished, I could have stayed at luxury hotels and eaten at gourmet restaurants, and many independent bicycle tourists do.

Actually, touring on your own, or with a few friends, is a wonderful way to discover a new region or country. Along the way you probably will test your limits with a few new challenges, and since your ride is unsupported, you *must* be a competent rider and able to handle minor repairs. And you undoubtedly will encounter some head winds and hills. Yet if you know the ropes, it's relatively easy and simple to plan and design a magnificent and rewarding tour.

How to Overcome the Language Problem

Many older people feel intimidated by foreign languages and cultures. How can you tour France if you don't speak French? After bicycling through every country in Western Europe except Finland, I've found that the following key phrases will serve in 90 percent of bicycle travel situations:

Please, I would like — .

Where is — ?

Thank you.

How much is it?

BIKECENTENNIAL PHOTO

Wyoming's Tetons provide a spectacular backdrop for cyclists on the Trans-America Bicycle Trail.

I/we need a room for one/two persons for one/two nights with (without) a private bath and toilet.

We shall leave at — in the morning. We shall need the door unlocked and our bicycles.

(That last phrase is because you cannot take your bicycle into your room in Europe and must leave it in a hotel storage area; also small European hotels often don't unlock the front door until 8 A.M.)

Have these phrases translated, and write them out phonetically, and you'll be able to travel almost anywhere in Europe. You should also learn the numbers up to 12. In any case, someone in most hotels usually speaks some English, while English is usually spoken in the tourist information office that exists in virtually every larger town in every resort area in Europe.

When touring independently, you must either: (1) travel light and stay at hotels or motels (or Bed & Breakfasts in England-Ireland) or at youth hostels; or (2) camp in a tent. Since tent camping means carrying at least 30 pounds of gear, and turning your bike into a beast of burden, I do not recommend it for a beginning adult tour. If you enjoy tent camping, it's better to join a group tour and have your tent and equipment carried on a truck. Instead, I will concentrate here on "light touring." This translates into carrying all your basic essentials in two pannier bags, and a handlebar or rack bag.

Racks and Touring Bags

I have carried quite heavy loads on the Pletscher aluminum racks. But for greater dependability, you should fit your bike with a triangular Blackburn rack.

A handlebar bag plus two standard-sized pannier bags should provide more than enough capacity for six weeks of hotel-motel touring or hostelling. It's best to avoid front panniers, which make the bike more difficult to steer and handle.

Most panniers are made of coated nylon stitched around a rigid internal frame, and they attach to the rack with a quick-mounting system. Each pannier has at least 3 outside pockets. Special panniers for mountain bike touring are also available that lock onto the top of the rack.

Handlebar bags attach to the handlebar with a quick-release system. They usually have a sturdy composite frame and come with front and side pockets and a map case. Mountain bike versions are also available. Everything you might need quickly should be carried in the handlebar bag along with camera, papers, and wallet. Whenever you leave the bike, take this bag with you.

Square-shaped rack bags to go atop your rack are also available should you need to carry more. Or you could use one in lieu of a handlebar bag. While they all are made of coated nylon, and have rain covers to protect the zippers, these bags are not entirely waterproof. Hence everything inside should be packed in large, strong plastic bags.

Travel Light

For light touring your total load should be well under 20 pounds. Except for tools, spares, and maps, you can usually pick up anything you forgot as you go along. Pack the heaviest items in the bottom of each bag. Never carry a rucksack, hip bag, or any other kind of bag on your person. Not only will the pack or bag raise your center of gravity and interfere with your balance, but it will also dig painfully into your body after a short time.

Choose everything for minimum weight. If you expect cool weather, take warm gloves, a sweater, windbreaker, and raingear. Carry long pants as well as shorts, and highly visible above-waist clothing. Incidentally, it's quite practical to bicycle in a pair of dark, wide-cut work pants, which you can also wear in hotels and restaurants. Keep your raingear in a pocket where you can get at it quickly.

Everyone has a personal list of what to take, but here are a few items I would prefer not to forget: a deep aluminum plate and camper's knife-fork-spoon set; can opener; metal cup; sunglasses; sewing kit; bandages; insect repellent; small flashlight; ten feet of nylon cord; and ample funds in travelers checks.

A single pair of bicycle touring shoes will see you through. Make sure you can walk comfortably in them. Avoid any plug-in electrical gadgets. For one thing, they won't work on the current in Europe or New Zealand.

Shipping Your Bicycle for Your Vacation Tour

Most airlines accept solo bikes but not all will take tandems. Nor can bicycles be carried on some smaller planes that serve small airports. Nonetheless, you can normally carry your bike as part of your baggage for around $30 each way on most domestic flights, and free on most international flights, provided it is counted as the larger of your two allowable suitcases. Its maximum permissible weight is 60–70 pounds.

Before choosing an airline to fly by, call and check its specifications for shipping bicycles. If you don't meet its requirements, your bicycle can be classed as excess baggage and charged a higher rate. For example, if you take a suitcase as well as a bike, the suitcase may be restricted to a total measurement of 55 inches.

Most airlines prefer your bicycle shipped in a box. If you can, get two bicycle boxes from a bike shop, one slightly larger than the other so that one can be used as a lid that slides over the other.

To pack, remove the saddle and post as a single unit; handlebar and stem, also as a single unit (and don't detach the brake cables); the front wheel; and the pedals. (The left-hand pedal has a left-hand thread.) Also unbolt the rear derailleur, partly deflate the tires, and shift all gears so that the cables are slack. Wrap all parts, together with the frame, in newspaper. Tape the front wheel to the center of the bike; tape the cranks parallel to the top tube; and tape the rear derailleur between the spokes of the rear wheel. Place a label on the bike giving your home and destination addresses and the flight number.

Insert the bike in the box and cradle in the handlebar and stem, the saddle and post, and the pedals. You can usually also pack in a tent, mattress, and sleeping bag, which will further help to protect the bike. To prevent the box from being crushed, insert sturdy pieces of cardboard to protect the quick-releases. Then cut two short pieces of 2 x 4″ lumber to act as internal braces and insert nails through the outside of the box to hold them in place. Secure the box tightly with tape or cord and place another label on the outside giving your home address, destination, and flight number.

Alternatively, you can pack your bike in a strong plastic bag or a special bicycle suitcase. A proper plastic shipping bag is fairly expensive, and the suitcase is quite expensive. They are sold by larger bike shops. However, if you can obtain a strong, well-padded plastic bag, you can pack your bike in that. Remove the front wheel and pedals, lower the saddle, and tape the handlebars parallel to the top tube. One advantage is that plastic bags are often stowed on top of suitcases and are less likely to be crushed.

Some airlines will accept an unprotected bike provided you sign a waiver of liability. If you ship a bike this way, you must remove the pedals and tape the handlebars parallel to the top tube. I'd also detach and remove the rear derailleur and pad the bike with foam wherever possible. Unprotected bikes can be easily scratched or damaged and the spokes broken.

Tips on Traveling with Your Bicycle

When you arrive at the overseas airport, your bicycle can be taken along with the rest of your baggage to the hotel where you spend your first night. Larger hotels have their own minibuses which meet arriving passengers and convey them, together with their bags, to the hotel. Alternatively, jitneys or airport buses exist which will usually drop you and your baggage at smaller hotels. If none of these is available, a taxi will always take you and your luggage (including your boxed bicycle) to the hotel at which you are staying.

BIKECENTENNIAL PHOTO BY GREG SIPLE

Bikecentennial's Great Parks North route in Glacier National Park takes cyclists through some of North America's most dramatic scenery.

Provided you spend your first and last nights overseas at the same hotel, you can invariably leave your bicycle box, bag or suitcase in the hotel's baggage room free of charge while you go on your tour.

On occasion, I have unboxed my bicycle at the airport, thrown away the box, and ridden out of the airport to commence my tour. In some cases, I've found that airlines provide boxes for the return flight. But they often run out and you may find that no boxes are actually available. Hence I prefer nowadays to store my bike box at a hotel until my return. Bike boxes are hard to find outside the United States. If you do plan to box your bike at the airport, take along some strong cord to fasten it with.

If you have a newer and an older bike, both equal in performance, take the older bike on your overseas vacation. If it's lost or damaged, you have less to lose. Mountain bikes are sturdier,

To ensure that your bicycle arrives at your destination with you, avoid tight connections. Try to fly all the way by the same airline. On some trips I have personally transferred the bike from one airline to another at a changeover airport by using a baggage pushcart. And do check in at the counter in plenty of time for the bike to be loaded.

If you're flying overseas, try to arrive at your destination 24 hours before your tour starts. This allows more time for your bike to get there. Some airlines have a much better reputation for handling bikes than others. I've found Air New Zealand to be exceptionally cooperative and the airline encourages passengers to bring bicycles.

Taking a Bicycle by Train or Bus

Amtrak will take boxed bikes as baggage on trains that have baggage compartments, but to ensure that the bike is at your destination when you arrive, I'd ship it a week ahead. You can also ship a boxed bike as baggage when you go by bus. Here again, I'd ship it 48 hours ahead of your own departure.

In Europe, New Zealand, and elsewhere, unprotected bicycles are accepted as baggage and they usually go either by the same train as you, or by a following train with a baggage car that usually arrives within 12 hours. There's one important caveat. When taking your bike on a train trip that requires crossing Paris, or any other large city, from one station to another, ship the bike only to the Paris arrival station. Ride it yourself across the city (or take a cab) to the departure station, and reship it for the onward journey. Otherwise, your bike—or any other luggage—can take a week to arrive.

Renting a bike on arrival might seem one way to avoid shipping it. But unless you are certain you will get a well-maintained multi-geared bike with low climbing gears and a frame that fits, don't consider renting. Some group tour operators can supply satisfactory bikes. And in mountain bike regions you may get a quality rental bike (but at a formidably high rent). Elsewhere, most rental bikes are clunkers or 3-speeds.

Where to Stay

There's absolutely no need to rough it when you go bicycle touring on your own. The oldest couple to bicycle around the world, Ken and Jaque Proctor, spent a million dollars during their recent nine-year tour of 150 countries, and they went deluxe all the way. Many older bicyclists who tour on their own prefer to stay at deluxe inns, lodges, resort hotels, dude ranches, and 4-star motels, and they dine in style every night.

However, most independent bicycle tourists prefer to stay at smaller economy motels in small towns. Virtually every American town with a population of 1,000 or more has at least one mom-and-pop-type motel. In the Sunbelt many of these are now operated by East Indian chains and each is managed by an East Indian family. They are comfortable, adequate, and inexpensive.

Additionally, in larger towns you'll find chain motels of the Motel Six, Motel Eight, Days Inns, Scottish Inns, Econo-Lodge, Ramada Inns, and other chains that offer a dependable level of comfort at a reasonable rate. Ramada Inns, Days Inns, Econo-Lodges and possibly others give a discount to bicyclists aged 60–62 or over.

One advantage of staying at motels in the United States is that you can take your bicycle into your room. This is not possible at Bed & Breakfast guest houses or hotels in Europe, nor at many motels in these countries. You must store your bike in an enclosed area outside, or else in the baggage room. So bring a small lock to secure it.

When to Make Advance Reservations

Out of season you can usually count on finding a motel room in any U.S. town of 5,000 or more if you arrive before 6 P.M. — that is, except on Saturdays, legal holidays, and during special events. I'd always have a confirmed reservation at these times. If you schedule one rest day per week, try to stay in the same place on both Friday and Saturday nights, thereby ensuring a room on the Saturday. Always have a first-night reservation for any destination to which you are flying. While touring you can phone ahead to make reservations on a day-to-day basis.

In some European countries, such as Ireland, Britain, Denmark, and Yugoslavia, you'll find tourist information offices in every resort town. For a nominal fee these offices will locate you a Bed & Breakfast room or a hotel room, in the price bracket you wish to pay. They will also phone ahead and reserve you a room at your next night's stopover. This room-finding service is not available in all countries. Yet virtually every town in Europe that is visited by tourists has an information office that will direct you to hotels, pensions, or guest houses that have vacancies in the price bracket you desire. In almost all these offices someone speaks English. Despite the language difference, traveling in Europe is often simpler than traveling in the United States.

Youth Hosteling

Few adults stay at youth hostels merely to save money. Two people can share a budget motel room in many parts of the United States, or an economy hotel room in Europe, for little more than the cost of staying at a youth hostel. Most adults stay at youth hostels because many of the hostels occupy unique locations in the hearts of scenic areas, and also for the opportunity to meet and mix with other bicyclists.

How many bicyclists, or other members of the fitness culture, have you ever met at a motel? Or have you ever found a motel in a lighthouse on the California Coast, or aboard a World War II battleship in Massachusetts, or on a ranch in the West? These are actual locations of some of the 250 youth hostels in the United States.

With an American Youth Hostels (AYH) membership you can stay at a friendly hostel in over 60 countries, mostly in cities or in scenic areas ideal for bicycling. The AYH is part of a worldwide network of hostels called the International Youth Hostels Federation, based in London. Most overseas hostels are in Europe, Australia, New Zealand, and Japan. Their locations and facilities are all listed in a series of handbooks available when you become a member.

The typical hostel provides dormitory-style accommodation, with separate rooms and bathrooms for men and women. Each dorm room accommodates 4–8 hostelers, but some hostels also have family rooms. There's a self-service kitchen where you can prepare your own meals, plus a dining area, and a common room where you can swap yarns with travelers from all over the world. Some hostels serve meals. All you need bring is a sheet sleeping bag and a washrag and towel. Most hostelers are asked to do a few volunteer household chores.

Although hostels tend to be crowded and noisy, many adults of all ages are avid hostelers. With the exception of Bavaria, and possibly

Switzerland, hostels in just about all other countries welcome bicyclists of all ages, both the young and the young-at-heart. The only caveat I would mention is to keep your valuables with you at all times. Bikes are usually kept in a bicycle shed where they should be locked.

Personally, I've enjoyed hosteling all over the world. Some hostels are in areas where economy-priced hotels and motels don't exist. And thousands of adults wouldn't travel any other way. Yet hosteling certainly isn't the only option for adults who go bicycling on their own.

Regrettably, many U.S. hostels close soon after Labor Day, at a time when weeks of good cycling weather remain. This is often not the case in Europe. I've toured Norway late in the season and had entire hostels to my group. And I once made a fantastic bike tour of England and Wales in February. With the exception of Saturday nights, my group were the sole guests at every hostel at which we stayed. Look up the address for American Youth Hostels in the Appendix.

When to Go Touring

Touring the United Kingdom in February might seem unrealistic. The days were short, we had some cold weather, and it did rain and blow. But there wasn't a single day on which we failed to cover at least 50 miles. We did not meet a single tourist and we had our pick of accommodations wherever we went. The only drawback for those staying at guest houses is that room-finding services are closed during the off-season. Out-of-season, you have to hunt up your own accommodations. In fact, in resort areas all over the world, many accommodations close between late fall and early spring, and in France many mom-and-pop hotels close for a vacation in late October.

Nonetheless, the best time to go bicycle touring is during the early and late seasons: between May 1 and July 2; and between Labor Day and early November. Both in Europe and the United States, the worst months are July and August. Tourists are swarming everywhere. Roads that are quiet in June and September are often full of cars in midsummer. And most accommodations are booked solid weeks in advance. Yes, you can do it, especially if you tent camp. But if you're light-touring, you should have confirmed reservations in all tourist areas.

Almost everywhere, late spring and early fall are the best seasons for bicycle touring. That includes Australia and New Zealand, where the seasons are the reverse of ours. You should also anticipate some extra weekend traffic during the fall color season in Colorado and New England.

For midwinter touring you might consider Hawaii, Baja California, Tasmania, New Zealand, and, in settled times, Sri Lanka. In the United States, the Texas Hill Country offers surprisingly good touring between November and April, although you can encounter occasional periods of wind and rain. Here again you should have confirmed reservations during the late-November to early-January hunting season.

Where to Get Maps for Your Tour

Most small-scale road maps used by motorists are useless for bicycle touring. You need large-scale maps that show the backroads and secondary routes that get you away from traffic.

Regardless of where you will tour in the United States, you should join Bikecentennial, a not-for-profit information, resource, and routing service for recreational bicyclists. Cofounded by Greg Siple, who with his wife and a group of other bicyclists rode from Alaska to Argentina in the 1970s, Bikecentennial maintains information on a 18,500 mile network of low-traffic secondary roads throughout the United States.

These include the Cross-Country Trans America Bicycle Trail, plus these routes: Canada to California; California coast; Maine to Virginia; Virginia to Florida; the Great Parks; Iowa to Maine; Washington to Minnesota; the Great River route; and a loop tour of Oregon. All are available in minute detail on water-resistant, state-of-the-art three-color maps designed to take you through the most beautiful parts of America at the perfect pace of bicycling.

Additionally, you receive *The Cyclist's Yellow Pages*, a complete guide to maps, books, routes, and organizations plus all national, regional, and overseas cycling organizations and travel information offices plus hundreds of invaluable facts such as which national parks and forests permit mountain bicycling.

You also receive the *Cyclosource Catalog*, a guide to the largest collection of current cycling information in the United States. Every regional bicycling guide and map, plus foreign guides and mountain biking guides, is listed and available from Bikecentennial. Membership also brings 9 issues of *Bike Report* magazine with descriptions of tours and day rides in the United States. Look up the address of Bikecentennial in the Appendix.

For U.S. county and topographical maps, see under "Maps to Take You Roaming in the United States" in Chapter 12.

Bicycling Maps for Touring Europe

For bicycling maps on the continent of Europe, write to Michelin Maps and Guides (address in Appendix) for a map and price list. Michelin makes detailed maps of France, Belgium, Luxembourg, The Netherlands, Portugal, Spain, Switzerland, Denmark, Morocco, Greece, and Yugoslavia.

Michelin's 35 regional maps of France and Corsica are incredibly detailed, each showing a labyrinth of quiet backroads that can take you almost anywhere without setting a wheel on a main highway. Each of *les Petites Routes* is smoothly paved, numbered, and clearly marked with signs. The Michelin series also includes maps of major cities and hotel guides to each country.

Other outstanding map series include Bartholomew's maps of the United Kingdom; Ordnance Survey maps of Ireland; the Shell Deutsche Generalkarte for Germany; the New Zealand Automobile Club maps of New Zealand; and the Australian Automobile Club maps of Australia. Maps for other countries can be had by phoning or writing to the respective national tourist offices listed in the *Cyclist's Yellow Pages* (or in the New York Yellow Pages). Free hotel guides are available from most national tourist offices, together with a map and general tourist information.

With the exception of New Zealand and Australia, don't depend on finding maps along the way during your tour. Frequently they are not available. Have all the maps you need *before* you leave home. That means advance planning. So begin planning and writing away for maps etc., at least three months before your tour. Don't forget, too, that you may need a visa for New Zealand, Australia, and possibly France, among other countries.

For a long tour of Europe I have carried as many as 35 maps, a fairly heavy load some three inches thick. As I used them, I mailed them home in packages of six.

Sightseeing

Unless you have a sizable group, you can't do much visiting of castles, museums, or cathedrals. That's because one member must always stay outside and watch the bikes. Even in super-honest

Ireland or Scandinavia, you can't leave expensive bicycles and bags unwatched. So if you expect a lot of sightseeing, you may want to reconsider going by bike.

In any event, take a light lock. You can also temporarily immobilize a bike by flipping the rear quick-release.

Never go into a café or store unless you can see your bike through the window. Otherwise, one member should stay outside and watch the bikes. Groups can take turns with each member guarding the bikes for five minutes.

You should also consider your companions. Are they inveterate sightseers, late risers, faster or slower than you, do they have different tastes or interests, or might they give up and leave you to ride on alone? For these reasons, many men or couples prefer to tour on their own and forgo sightseeing.

How Far Should You Ride?

For light touring, the *maximum* average distance should be 85 miles per day on fairly level terrain, 75 miles in hilly country, and 65 miles in mountains or when carrying camping gear. Really fit people can maintain these distances for at least six days each week.

For those who prefer to browse and stop for snacks or coffee along the way, half these distances can be ample. Learn your own daily mileage capability and select overnight stops to dovetail with the distance you can ride.

However, no one should consider touring independently unless able to ride at least 50 miles a day without getting tired. You might also consider what would happen if a strong headwind prevents you from reaching your planned destination for the day. One good reason for touring in the off-season is that alternative accommodation is easy to find.

Best Touring Areas at Home and Abroad

As a very rough guide to some of the best touring areas I have experienced, here are a few comments.

United States and Canada

• *Alaska.* Good biking exists in south central Alaska, especially from Anchorage through the Copper River Valley and by ferry to Columbia Glacier and Whittier, thence by train back to Anchorage.

- *Arizona.* The Grand Canyon country is popular with many, both North and South Rims. Be prepared for traffic.
- *California.* Good riding exists in Guerneville and the Russian River country; Alexander Valley; Bodega Bay; Mother Lode country; Delta Region; Point Reyes Seashore; Napa Valley and the Silverado Trail; Monterey Peninsula; the Redwood Country and Eureka; and the Pacific Coast.
- *Colorado.* Exciting mountain scenery exists through the Rockies. Try Boulder to Estes Park via Raymond-Allenspark thence Trail Ridge, Grand Lake, Idaho Springs, Mount Evans, Golden, and through Arvada to Boulder. Or try Golden to Vail via the bike route over Loveland Pass and the Vail Pass bike path, thence to Glenwood Springs, Independence Pass, Leadville, Dillon, and via Loveland Pass back to Golden. Best immediately after Labor Day.
- *Hawaii.* Circumnavigate the Big Island of Hawaii from Hilo to Waimea, the Kohala Peninsula, Hawaii Volcanoes National Park and back along the north Kona Coast. Expect some traffic.
- *Massachusetts.* Cape Cod, Martha's Vineyard and Nantucket offer short, easy touring, but go during the off-season to avoid traffic.
- *Montana and Wyoming.* These two are top bicycle touring states.
- *New Hampshire.* You'll find lots of good cycling and scenery in this delightful New England state.
- *New York.* The Finger Lakes country is perennially popular.
- *North Carolina.* This is probably the best bicycle touring state in the South.
- *Oregon.* From Astoria to Brookings, US 101 hugs the Pacific, taking you over rugged headlands and past hundreds of miles of wild seascapes and surging ocean. Many state parks offer camping, there are plenty of accommodations, and the best time is immediately after Labor Day. Although shoulders are wide enough most of the way, traffic is fairly constant and includes a mix of logging trucks and RVs.
- *Pennsylvania.* Lancaster County, with its Amish farms and covered bridges, is the popular favorite, but I've bicycled through much of northern Pennsylvania and enjoyed it.
- *Texas.* The Hill Country, bordered by San Antonio, Austin, Ozona, Uvalde, and Llano, offers hundreds of miles of lightly traveled backroads for all-season touring. Best in spring and late fall (summer afternoons are hot). County road maps are essential. Big

BIKECENTENNIAL PHOTO BY RICH LANDERS

Bicycle camper touring in the northern Cascades of Washington state.

Bend National Park offers rugged mountain bike touring. West
Texas also has good road touring in the fall.

• *Utah.* For a superbly scenic desert and mountain tour go from
Cedar City to Cedar Breaks National Monument, Panguitch, Bryce
Canyon National Park, Escalante, Boulder, Torrey, Capitol Reef
National Park, Hanksville, Natural Bridges National Monument
and Blanding via some of the most dramatic scenery in the United
States. You need a tent, it's hot in summer. A fantastic ride over-
looked in the stampede to Grand Canyon. Big hills.

• *Vermont.* A major bicycling touring state full of winding country lanes, historic villages and country inns. The Champlain Valley,
the still-wild Northeast Kingdom, the Connecticut River Valley,
and the mountains of central and southern Vermont all offer appealing touring and mountain biking opportunities.

• *Washington.* The San Juan Islands, reached by ferry from An-
acortes, offer easy, hassle-free touring.

• *Canadian Rockies.* The Banff, Lake Louise, Jasper and Icefields
Parkway region offers grand bicycle touring on wide shoulders with
glaciers, peaks, elk, moose and black bear. You can camp or stay at
resort accommodations. Start your tour as soon as possible after
September third, which is approximately when the main tourist
season ends. (I very strongly suggest arriving in Banff not later than
September fourth and starting your tour the following day.) The
off-season is quite brief, and it can get really cold toward the end of
September.

Europe

Distances are short, few towns are more than 25 miles apart, and
most of Europe north of the Alps is honeycombed with backroads.
There is little trash or broken glass, and few loose dogs. Go in late
spring or early fall.

• *Austria.* You can cycle through famous wine regions in flatter
eastern Austria, and also continue into Hungary. Expect some
traffic.

• *Denmark.* This delightful country is mostly flat and covered
with backroads and bike paths. Stay in *kros* (rural inns), explore
Jutland, the west coast, and the town of Ribe. From Copenhagen
you can ferry over to Sweden and return to Denmark at Helsingor.

• *France.* In my estimation, this is the world's top bicycling touring country. Good regions are Alsace, the Rhine and Vosges; Nor-
mandy and Brittany; the Loire Valley; the Alps and Provence; south

central and southwestern France; and Corsica. Avoid large centers, stay in small towns, dine sumptuously at local bistros and stay at inexpensive hotels or atmospheric hostelries of the Relais et Chateaux group. Out of season, Corsica resembles one big national park. There are lots of hills everywhere in France plus fast trains that carry bikes, and superb cycling on the world's most extensive, fully paved backroads system.

- *Germany.* Bavaria is the favorite region, a land of alpine peaks, castles, and medieval towns. The Black Forest is also pleasant out of season, and I have enjoyed cycling in north Germany, Lunenberge Heide, the Romantische Strasse and along the Moselle. Expect some traffic.

- *Ireland.* Out of season, the entire coast, plus the interior of Ireland, is a bicyclist's paradise. Riding over the great headlands and peninsulas is sheer joy. So is cycling through the glistening mountains of Connemara, and circling the Ring of Kerry, looking down on vast seascapes of golden bays and pebble beaches. Full of friendly pubs where you can hear the silvery-tongued rhetoric. Avoid July and August, bring your raingear.

- *Italy.* The hills of Tuscany and Umbria, the region around Bologna, and the Veneto region (including Verona, Padua, and Vicenza) offers good backroads bicycling. But expect some traffic and avoid large cities.

- *The Netherlands.* Networked with *fietspads*, you must learn the rules for riding these bike lanes. They have their own traffic lights and signs. Bike bells, lights and reflectors are required by law. A bicycling mecca for the easy rider with gardens full of flowers, and *fietspads* that run along the dikes, the Netherlands is a picturesque and pleasant place for a beginners' tour.

- *Norway.* Smooth but largely unpaved roads offer great bicycling. Early September is best. Take a mountain bike with road tires, warm clothes, raingear, and lots of money. It's frequently wet, cool and overcast—but don't miss it!

- *Portugal.* Northern Portugal remains one of Europe's most colorful and unspoiled regions with great rides between such towns as Viano do Castelo, Calheiros, Braga, Guimaräes, and Vieira do Minhos, and through the provinces of Douro and Minho. Expect some traffic and watch for cobblestone roads. A mountain bike with road tires is probably best.

- *Spain.* Galicia, in northwest Spain, is a timeless region that adjoins northern Portugal. You can stay at deluxe, historic *paradores* or at a choice of inexpensive hotels.

- *Switzerland.* Northwest Switzerland resembles France's adjoining Haute Savoie and offers good hilly biking. But there are relatively few roads in the Alps and they are full of cars.
- *United Kingdom.* The farther from London, the better the bicycling. Stay on the backroads and off the main roads. The Cotswolds are the most popular bicycling area but Cornwall, Scotland, Ulster, and west Wales offer beautiful backroads touring. East Anglia has flat riding for the easy rider. Room-finding services and Bed & Breakfast guest homes are most numerous on the coasts and in resort areas. Nontourist areas may not have much accommodation.

Other Countries

- *Australia.* You'll find good bicycling in the island state of Tasmania with lots of hills and campgrounds. Expect some traffic. I also found interesting mountain bicycling around Cooma, Mount Beauty, Bright, and other towns in the Snowy Mountains of Victoria. There are plenty of inexpensive motels and campgrounds. But on the mainland, paved highways are relatively few and unsuited for touring. Biking in Australia is most worthwhile if done in conjunction with a tour of New Zealand. A mountain bike with road tires is best.
- *New Zealand.* Resembling Scotland, the South Island is one of the world's best bicycle touring areas. Take a mountain bike with road tires as there are also many unpaved roads worth exploring. Go down the West Coast from Picton to Nelson, Murchison, Westport, Greymouth, Franz Josef Glacier, Fox Glacier, Haast Pass, Lake Moeraki, and Queenstown to Fiordland National Park and beyond. There are plenty of good campgrounds but motel rooms may be hard to find during the December-March tourist season. There are also comfortable inns, hotels, and fishing lodges. Go in early or late season, or in midseason if you are tenting. Highly recommended, but bring raingear and warm clothes. It rains heavily on the West Coast; use mudguards. Do not use skinny tires. Some dirt road riding is inescapable though most routes are paved. 27 x 1¼" tires or comparable 700 sizes will get you through.
- *Bali, Indonesia.* Best taken in our midsummer, a mountain bike tour of the island of Bali is becoming increasingly popular. Expect extreme heat and humidity but grand scenery. It's about 260 miles around the island via Sanur, Legian, Bedugul, Lovina Beach, Penelokan, Candidasa and Ubud. Expect traffic. Safe but adventurous;

allow ten days or more. This tour can be done at any time, but rain is heavier in our winter season.

• *Guatemala.* I have enjoyed magnificent touring in the Guatemala Highlands away from Guatemala City. Take a mountain bike with road tires. Most places have comfortable hotels. Expect some traffic. Grand scenery. Adventurous.

• *India.* I have enjoyed bicycling in the Himalayas starting from Rishikesh, north of Delhi. Take a mountain bike with road tires. Light traffic, hilly. Adventurous.

• *Nepal.* From Kathmandu you can tour much of Nepal, riding to the Tibetan border and all over the highland area. Take a mountain bike. It's possible to mountain bicycle on some of the main trekking routes. It's best to tent camp. Safe, but hilly and adventurous. Mountain bike rentals in Kathmandu can be arranged in advance through Narain Getaways to Nepal, 948 Pearl St., Boulder CO 80302, phone 303-440-0331.

• *Sri Lanka.* Once the political situation calms down, Sri Lanka should become one of the most pleasant and attractive countries for adventure touring. Ride around the southwest coast and return through the interior via Kandy and Nuwara Eliya. Flat on coast, big hills in interior.

CHAPTER 14

Escorted Bicycle Tours— Freewheeling Vacations by Pedal Power

*O*ne way to ensure getting hooked on bicycling is to take an easy-paced group tour designed for beginners.

As John Freidin, founder of Vermont Bicycle Touring once told me: "Everyone in good health can enjoy recreational bicycling. Nearly half of our bicyclists take their first bicycle trip with us. After just a weekend, they're hooked!"

Anyone who can ride 30 miles a day can qualify for a variety of comfortable bicycle adventure tours. Today, over 100 organizations offer group tours ranging from a weekend to a week or a month or longer.

In New England, California, or Europe, both younger and older bicyclists enjoy touring on scenic routes from one elegant country inn to another, with fine dining, and a support van (called a sag wagon) to carry the luggage and pick up stragglers.

In fact, bicycle touring has become trendy. You can choose from deluxe bicycle tours that take you first class all the way, with part of the tour on a schooner cruise or at a beach resort in Hawaii, with cocktails before dinner, and with sumptuous dining every night. Some bike tours include summer theater, tennis, dancing, swimming, or music festivals as part of their trips. Group bicycle tours are organized primarily for beginning and intermediate riders, not for ironmen, and emphasis is on having a great time outdoors. However, purists who want to pedal nonstop all day are not overlooked. Most tours offer three optional routes on each day's ride.

Beginners can take the easy route, averaging 20–35 miles; more seasoned riders can take the intermediate route, averaging 35–50 miles; and advanced riders can take the high road through challenging terrain for 60–80 miles or more. In late afternoon, everyone arrives at the same hotel or inn for refreshments and dinner.

Regardless which route you take, you go at your own pace. You can ride on your own, or with a friend or a small group. On the average tour, participants are strung out for miles and no one has to "keep up." If you like frequent stops for snacks or sightseeing, you can choose the short, flat route that allows ample time to dawdle at antique shops and art galleries. In fact, some people ride only as far as the lunch stop, and go the rest of the way in the sag wagon.

Active Tours for Dedicated Bicyclists

Meanwhile, more experienced riders can ride a more demanding route that really challenges their bicycling abilities.

Certainly, the trend today is away from long camping tours to shorter ten-day tours with comfortable accommodations where you can pay for meals with a credit card. But opportunities for more rigorous, and slightly more spartan, tours at lower cost are still

COURTESY: BACKCOUNTRY BICYCLE TOURS

A tour group enjoys a break in Wyoming's Grand Teton National Park.

there. Outfits like Bikecentennial offer a choice of superb camping tours that take you roaming for two or three months completely across the United States or the length of the Pacific Coast, or from Montana to Alaska.

Meanwhile, American Youth Hostels offers an exciting World Adventure Program that includes long bike tours through the Canadian Rockies, New Zealand, Europe, and all over the United States, at rockbottom cost. Several hosteling tours are open only to riders over 50, while adults of any age can join any of their tours which are classified as "open" or "adult." Some of these tours have had leaders who themselves were age 65.

Among the advantages of joining a group tour is the opportunity to meet other bicyclists. Nothing breeds camaraderie more than a shared experience, and an extraordinary closeness soon develops among a cycling group. Numerous friendships are almost guaranteed. On one Vermont Bicycle Tours trip, a couple met and were married and the rest of their tour became their honeymoon.

Insouciant Touring

Joining a group tour also relieves busy people of the chores of planning routes and making reservations. All reservations are confirmed months in advance while the tour operator takes care of all details and guarantees a successful trip. All you need do is to relax and enjoy the ride.

Almost all medium and higher cost tours provide sag wagon support. The van carries luggage, spare parts, tools, and refreshments. It will pick up anyone wishing to cycle only part of the day, or who feels tired. Later, the van will sweep the route for stragglers. However, sag wagon support is usually confined only to easy and intermediate routes. Advanced riders are expected to be self-sufficient, although the van will always go out and pick up anyone who phones to the overnight stop for help.

On commercial tours, the leaders or sag wagon drivers double as mechanics, and they'll keep your bicycle running in the event of mechanical trouble.

All this doesn't come cheap. In 1990 rates for a deluxe tour, with overnights at historic inns and sag support, averaged $90 per day in the United States, and ranged up to $150 per day for overseas tours, including air fare. Single-occupancy rates can add 15–35 percent more. While these costs cover accommodation, breakfast, dinner, maps, taxes, sag support, and the services of a professional leader, you could easily halve these rates by touring on your own at the economy level.

Adventure Tours at Lower Cost

Meanwhile, if you enjoy camping or hosteling, or are willing to ride without sag support, not-for-profit organizations like Bikecentennial or the AYH, plus other outdoor clubs and organizations, offer well-organized adventure tours at rates far below those of the commercial tour operators.

In this not-for-profit category is the Bicycle Adventure Club, which operates adult-only group tours in the United States and overseas, with sag support and comfortable accommodations, but you pay only what the tour actually costs. Leaders are volunteers and each has scouted the route beforehand.

Which reminds me of a caveat: often, an enthusiastic bicyclist will offer to lead a group tour through an area that he or she has not scouted, nor even been to before. While the majority of such trips are offered through local bike clubs and are not-for-profit, the leader is often rewarded by being given a free trip. Most of these trips are well-intentioned and may use sag support and comfortable accommodations with advance reservations. But the leader is virtually going blind. I have seen such trips follow poorly planned itineraries that missed the best roads and scenery. Too, inexperienced leaders can encounter difficulties, such as unexpected national holidays, which can completely upset the group's plans. So make sure your tour leader is familiar with the area and has made the trip at least once before.

Your Fellow Tour Members

On the typical light bicycle tour half the participants are aged over 40. In fact, the longer and more expensive the tour, the higher the average age level. That's obviously because younger people can't take the time off from work for tours of three weeks or longer, nor can the majority afford it. While most commercial tours are open to anyone 21 or over, participants on long thirty-day tours of New Zealand, Nepal, Europe, or the Soviet Union are likely to be mature adults who have the time and finances to go. Statistics show that ages on the typical tour range from 22 to 66 with many riders in their 60s and some in their 70s.

The average group tour numbers 15–25 participants and represents a mix of singles, couples, families, and friends. On shorter tours as many as half the participants may be singles, with women often outnumbering men. Most tour clients are affluent, college-educated professionals who are active and fit but more into recreational bicycling than racing.

Several organizations have offered tours exclusively for women (Womantrek, Outdoor Women's School, Calypso Excursions, and others) while Michigan Bicycle Tours has operated trips exclusively for vegetarians.

If you're a purist, and prefer to ride all day and go fairly long distances, you'll find a number of operators who specialize in fairly strenuous tours for real bicycling buffs. Frequently, the conversation is all about bicycles and equipment, and many of the riders are experienced veterans who have toured all over the world. Bicycle Adventure Club tends to be in this league.

Preplanned Independent Tours

Most tour operators will also arrange a completely planned independent tour in which you can ride on your own, or take along a group of friends. The tour operator does all the planning and makes all reservations. All you do is follow the routing instructions and keep to the schedule. If your group is large enough, you can also have your own sag wagon with driver. Costs are about the same as for the operator's standard group tours.

In Chapter 12, I recommended bringing your own high-performance bicycle if you can. But to avoid the hassle of flying with a bike, many tour participants rent bicycles from the tour operator. Rental bikes supplied by tour operators are usually dependable, well-maintained machines with rates that run about $15 a day. Some operators also rent mountain bikes for around $90 per week.

I'd avoid renting from anyone but a tour operator or mountain bike rental firm. Meanwhile, if you can drive to the starting point of your tour, I still recommend bringing your own bike.

Locating Bicycle Tour Operators

Several organizations publish source lists of all bicycle tour operators at least once a year. Among the best sources are:

- *League of American Wheelmen* (address in Appendix). By joining the L.A.W., you receive the bimonthly *Bicycle USA* magazine, the March-April issue of which gives details on virtually every bicycle tour operator plus operators of youth tours, self-guided tours, and mountain bike tours.

• *Bikecentennial* (address in Appendix). As a member you receive the *Cyclist's Yellow Pages*, which also gives brief listings of all leading bike tour operators, with addresses and phone number, and tells where they go.

COURTESY: VERMONT BICYCLE TOURING

At the Three Stallion Inn, Randolph, Vermont. Vermont is one of the most popular destinations for escorted inn-to-inn tours.

Several bicycling magazines also feature a run-down of tour operators in early spring issues while their back pages are often filled with ads by leading tour operators.

To give you an idea of the kinds of tours available, here is a brief listing of some of the largest bicycle tour operators and where their tours go.

Leading Bicycle Tour Operators

• *American Youth Hostels* (address in Appendix). Adult or Senior membership entitles you to an extensive choice of semiadventurous hosteling tours through Alaska, New England, Europe, the Canadian Rockies, the Pacific Coast, the Northeast, Colorado, the Southwest, and New Zealand.

• *Bicycle Adventure Club*, P.O. Box 87483, San Diego CA 92138 (619-273-2602). A not-for-profit membership touring club for adult bicyclists with tours to New Zealand, France, Germany, Eastern Europe, New England, Northern California, the United Kingdom, and many other areas.

• *Bikecentennial* (address in Appendix). Offers a series of inexpensive, self-contained camping tours that typically include a 90-day, 4,500 mile Across America trip; a 70-day 3,200-mile tour from Montana to Alaska; a 48-day, 2,150-mile tour from Oregon to Colorado; and many others. Bikecentennial also offers top-notch tours for mountain bicyclists, and also for road riders preferring indoor accommodations. All road rides follow the National Bicycle Route Network.

• *Bike Vermont*, P.O. Box 207TK, Woodstock VT 05091 (802–457-3553). Specializes in tours of Vermont.

• *Back Country Bicycle Tours*, PO Box 4029, Bozeman MT 59772 (406-586-3556). Mountain bike tours in Montana, Yellowstone, the Tetons, Utah, and New Zealand.

• *Backroads Bicycle Touring*, PO Box 1626, San Leandro CA 94577 (415-895-1783). Deluxe California wine country tours plus 30 different itineraries through North America, Europe, and the Pacific including Hawaii, Bali, and New Zealand. Stresses creature comforts, gourmet food.

• *Butterfield and Robinson*, 70 Bond Street, Toronto ONT Canada M5B 1X3 (in United States 800-387-1147; in Canada

800-268-8415). Top-quality bike tours through France, Italy, England, Ireland, Germany, Denmark, Austria, Spain, and Portugal.
• *China Passage,* 168 State Street, Teaneck NJ 07666 (201-837-1400). Tours of China when available and of Thailand, with sightseeing.
• *International Bicycle Tours,* 12 Mid-Place, Chappaqua NY 10514 (914-238-4576). Tours through the U.S.S.R., Denmark, Holland, Yugoslavia, and Bermuda, most personally led by president Frank Behrendt.
• *Vermont Bicycle Touring,* Box 711, Bristol VT 05443 (802-453-4811). Inn-to-inn tours of 2–21 days for beginners, intermediate, and advanced bicyclists through rural New England. Also operates tours through Britain, Hawaii, and New Zealand.

CHAPTER 15

How to Break into Competitive Bicycling

*I*f you like to ride for the thrill of competing, you'll find lots of action in Masters cycling.

Adult racers are classed as Masters if aged 30 or over, and as Seniors if aged 29 or under. Seven hundred Masters riders registered for the road and time trials, and 200 for track events, in the 1988 National Masters Championships.

The United States is also considered the world's best country for women racers. Scores of women riders like Jeannie Longo of France, Marianne Berglund of Sweden, and Maria Canins of Italy have trained and raced in the United States because women are discouraged from racing in Europe. In the United States women can compete with men, and some women have already beaten men's records.

Beginning Masters racing is easy to enter while older men and women can work up to the National Senior Olympics and win a gold medal.

Although competition is plentiful up to the Masters-50 age level, after that it begins to taper off. When Fred Knoller of Fort Lauderdale, Florida, became Grand Master of the United States in his mid-80s, he was forced to compete against himself in time trials because there was no other rider in his age bracket at that time. A vegetarian for decades, Fred rode his time trial for several years as part of the Coors Classic events.

Phil Guarnacia of Santa Ana, California, recently aged 73, finds plenty of competition by riding against men 20 and 30 years his junior. And Allen Ashmore, who took up bicycling at age 48 to lose weight, soon found that he could go so far and so fast that he began to race. Ten years later, at age 58, he typically competes in two Masters races in a day and had recently become the Masters National Road Champion in the 55-plus age group.

Vic Copeland was another rider who took up racing in his 40s after watching his son Zac race. In 1988, both Vic and Zac were National Criterium Champions.

Seniors or Masters Racing

The first step is to contact local bicycle clubs and bike shops and obtain the location of the nearest USCF bicycle racing club. Then find out what races the club offers, especially in your class, whether that is Senior or Master. Last, consider how far you must drive to reach the club's events. Most racers can probably manage to drive 75–100 miles but driving farther soon becomes a drag.

Over 1,100 bicycle racing clubs in the United States are coordinated by the U.S. Cycling Federation (USCF), the governing body behind amateur bicycle racing in the United States. Through these clubs the USCF promotes almost all USCF-sanctioned bicycle races in this country. Each local club is run by men and women who for the most part are in the Masters age group. Hence these adult members organize frequent Masters races for themselves. Thus virtually all Masters racing is promoted through local USCF-coordinated clubs.

The USCF classifies Seniors into four categories, ranging from category 4, beginners, to category 1, riders in national competition. But Masters cycling is graded by age. At all local level races, the organizers are free to use any age groups they wish. Only for District and National Masters races are specific age classes set up.

In most local Masters competitions ten-year classes are used, starting at age 30. Thus you typically find men's classes from 30–39, from 40–49, from 50–59 and from 60 up. Age groups for women are typically 30–39, 40–49, and 50 up. When not all age classes can be covered, extra prizes are usually awarded within the oldest age class. For example, there will be a prize for the fastest male rider over 65, over 70, and over 75; and for the fastest woman rider over 55, over 60, and so on.

"Honking" up a hill by standing on the pedals is a racing technique being used here by cyclists in the annual Tour of Ohio's Scioto River Valley. Nowadays, over twenty-five percent of the participants in this famous cycling event are over 40.

Besides organizing local, district, and sectional race meets, the USCF Masters Committee holds a National Championship annual meeting that includes a Masters road race, a time trial, a criterium championship, and track events. Each year, they also hold bicycle races as part of the Senior Olympics.

The Senior Olympics

The U.S. National Senior Olympics began in 1987 and is now held annually. To compete you must be 55 or over. During the first year over 2,800 athletes participated in events in bicycling, swimming, running, golf, and other sports.

To compete in the Senior Olympics you must qualify at sanctioned regional bicycle races held in March and April. They typically consist of 1-mile, 1-kilometer, 5-kilometer, 10-kilometer, and 20-kilometer races.

If an active USCF racing club is within reach, and you have decided to go in for competitive bicycling, write or phone the USCF (address in Appendix) and obtain an annual racing license. The USCF also publishes a rule book covering all requirements from clothing to riding, and it also has publications on all aspects of racing.

To obtain a racing license you must be a U.S. citizen or legal resident, and to enter a sanctioned race you must wear an approved helmet and black cycling shorts. Currently over 30,000 amateur racers hold USCF licenses, mostly in the Junior and Senior categories.

The USCF also publishes *Cycling USA*, which features a Masters column each month. It is packed with racing news and includes a racing calendar with information on all upcoming races and meets. *Cycling USA* also carries information on the Senior Olympics.

Other bicycle racing newspapers and magazines exist, including *Velo-News*, which also carries an extensive list of upcoming races. However, these are not official USCF publications. A good source of books on racing is the Vitesse Press (address in the Appendix B).

Races themselves are divided into road events and track events. Within each category is a variety of specialized and varied races.

In the United States the most popular road events are road races, criterium races, and time trials.

- *Road races* vary from 10 to 100 miles or more. They are held on streets or highways shared with traffic and often include long hills.

Road races may run from one point to another, or they may consist of several laps around a large loop. Most Senior road races are for at least 50 miles. Some are run in two or more stages and they may extend over two or more days. Competitors ride road-racing bicycles and their speed averages about 25–30 m.p.h. Such consistently high speeds are achieved by riding in a pack and drafting each other.

• *Criterium races* are held on a level course of two miles or less over which the competitors ride approximately 100 laps for a total distance of 60–100 kilometers. These are fast-paced rides in which the competitors often stay bunched together until the final sprint. Speeds vary from 25 to 30 m.p.h., which results in tight, fast cornering and frequent spills. Since the riders pass constantly in front of the spectators at high speed, the criterium has become the most popular road event in the United States.

• A *time trial* means riding against the clock over a fixed distance, usually 10–25 miles. Riders do not compete, pace, draft each other, or ride together. Riders leave at intervals of one minute, and attempt to maintain a speed so high that they are totally exhausted at the moment of crossing the finish line. The rider making the fastest time is the winner.

Another variation of the time trial requires each participant to ride as far as possible in a fixed time. The rider covering the longest distance wins. Some of these time trials last 24 hours. The world record for a 24-hour time trial is over 500 miles at an average speed of 21 m.p.h.

Team time trials are another variation in which teams of four riders compete. Each rider usually stays in the lead for a minute, before dropping back. The team making the fastest time wins.

Since most races must be ridden on roads shared with traffic, local clubs frequently organize time trials so that riders can train without having to ride in a pack.

Less popular nowadays are other types of road events, such as "miss and out" races in which, say at every fifth lap, the last rider must drop out; and "points" races in which the winner is the rider who scores the highest total of points awarded for making the fastest time in each lap, and for being ahead in each lap, and so on.

• A *stage race* consists of a series of races, usually including time trials, road races, and criteriums, held over a period of several days. The winning rider is the one with the lowest total elapsed time for all events.

An alternative method of scoring is to award points for the first three places in each race, and these are totaled instead. Additional points may be awarded for the first to finish a certain criterium lap, or for the fastest time up a major climb. The world's most famous stage race is the Tour de France, which occupies 3 full weeks.

Track Races

Since track races are ridden on special fixed-wheel bicycles without brakes, we recommend your gaining experience in road competition before considering track riding. Track races are short and fast and often include some type of pursuit or sprint. They are held on closed, banked tracks known as velodromes and winning depends as much on strategy as on speed.

Mountain Bicycle Races

The governing body for off-road bicycle races is the National Off-Road Bicycle Association (NORBA), which recently became associated with USCF. To compete in all but small, local mountain bicycle races, riders must be licensed by NORBA. Mountain bicycle racing is a highly specialized sport and mountain racing bikes are quite expensive. It's best to start out in entry level races using a regular mountain bicycle to see how you like it.

Triathlons

Over 2,000 triathlons of varying levels of challenge are held annually in the United States. Unlike the Ironman events, in which typically contestants swim 1–2 miles, run a marathon, and then ride a century, the average triathlon is based on a 1,500-meter swim, a 6-mile run, and a 25-mile bicycle ride.

There are also Masters triathlons, which typically call for swimming 800 meters, running or racewalking 5 miles, and bicycling 15 miles. Although this might sound super-strenuous, it is well within the capabilities of many fit 60-year-olds.

Triathlons are frequently announced by all local swimming, running, bicycling, and athletic clubs; by bicycle and sports gear shops; and also in the monthly state bicycling publications that are appearing in most bicycle-oriented states, and that are usually available free of charge at bicycle shops. In Texas, for example, forthcoming

triathlons are listed in *Texas Bicyclist,* a monthly tabloid-size publication carrying announcements of virtually all bicycle activities in
the state. Biathlons are also listed. (A biathlon usually combines
bicycling and running or bicycling and swimming).

Fitness Counts More than an Expensive Bicycle

In entry-level racing, equipment is less important than fitness. To
begin racing you need only to be able to ride smoothly and to have
good reflexes, a reasonable level of fitness, and the desire to
compete.

As described in Chapter 4, you can begin racing at the local level
on a sports bike by changing to lightweight tires and removing any
rack or other nonessential equipment. All you then need is a helmet
and black cycling shorts. If you find you enjoy racing, you can
upgrade your bike with lightweight rims and change to clipless
pedals and cycling shoes. Or you can buy a brand new racing bike.
A good medium-quality racing bike costs no more than a mountain
bike.

The secret of racing success lies in fitness, strategy and determina-
tion. You don't need an expensive Italian racing bike.

Finding Out Your Strengths and Weaknesses

As early in the game as possible you should ascertain your
strengths and weaknesses. Older riders frequently do better in long-
distance races than in short, fast events. A mature rider with good
stamina can often make a good showing in long road races.

If you're stocky and muscular you'll probably excel in fast flat
races. Or if you're lean and tall, you'll probably do better in long,
hilly road races.

Meanwhile, you can work at strengthening your weaknesses by
riding in criteriums and time trials. To succeed in criteriums you
must be a good sprinter and able to ride in a tight, fast pack. And to
succeed in time trials calls for the ability to pedal as hard as possible
for periods of an hour or more.

What It Takes

To succeed in Masters racing most adult riders need to develop
their endurance, power, and bike-handling abilities. You can do
this by riding far, fast, and frequently. Most Masters racers train by
using interval training as described in Chapter 8. It's seldom worth

having a coach. But as you get further into racing you will need a support person to hand you food and water during races, and to have replacement wheels on hand in case you get a flat.

At every opportunity you should ride in training races offered by racing clubs. You must learn to ride smoothly in a pack, and how to briefly sit on another rider's wheel while you regain enough energy to either overtake him or her, or to sprint around and cross the finish line first.

If there's one secret to winning races, it is this ability to conserve your energy for the last few minutes of a race by drafting the pack, or by briefly drafting another individual rider.

While it is perfectly legal to sit on another rider's wheel throughout a race, doing so for more than a brief time is considered unsportsmanlike. Nonetheless, many riders rely on this type of strategy to win. While the rider ahead exhausts his or her energy, these riders still have enough left to make a final sprint for the finish line.

How to Ride in a Pack

During road races all riders generally ride together in a close, tight pack (called a *peloton*) to help overcome the resistance of headwinds. Sometimes, there can be over 100 riders in a peloton. Approximately once each minute the leaders peel off and drop back while the riders immediately behind them take the lead position for the next 60 seconds. By riding flat out for one minute, they can keep the pack's speed at 30 m.p.h. or more. This cuts wind resistance for the riders trailing behind by at least 20 percent. Riding in the rear of a large pack is like riding behind a semitrailer.

All riders in a pack are expected to work up to the front and become a leader for about a minute. However, in a large, mixed peloton consisting predominantly of Seniors with a sprinkling of Masters, older riders are not obligated to take the lead. If they do, they often make only a dozen strong pedal revolutions before turning left and dropping back to the rear of the peloton.

Whether riding in a large pack, or drafting another rider, you must be constantly alert. You must ride smoothly even while changing gear or braking. Your front wheel is often only a foot or so behind that of the rider you're drafting. Should that rider slow, you must veer to one side or gently apply your brakes.

Because braking should be avoided while riding in a pack, it's safest not to follow directly behind the wheel ahead but to keep your front wheel a few inches to one side or the other. In case the rider ahead slows, you can then soft-pedal rather than use your brakes. Braking upsets the pattern of riders behind you.

Even though you may be drafting only a single rider, this can cut the effort you must put into pedaling by 15–20 percent and even more at higher speeds. Should the wind be diagonal to your path, riders stretch out at an angle known as an *echelon*, creating a diagonal formation resembling that of a flight of geese.

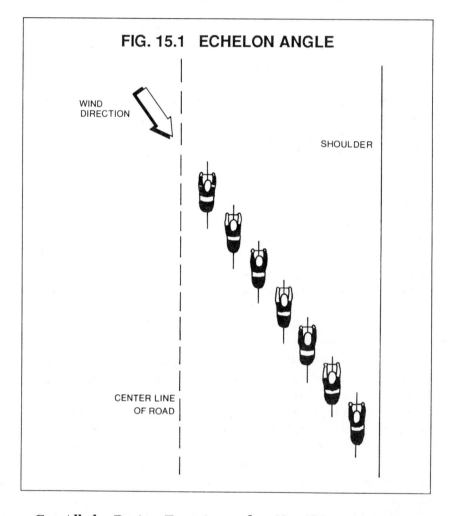

FIG. 15.1   ECHELON ANGLE

WIND DIRECTION

SHOULDER

CENTER LINE OF ROAD

Get All the Racing Experience that You Can

To gain experience, ride as often as possible in training rides, and in time trials and weekend races held by your local racing club. To encourage beginners, most clubs sponsor races and time trials for novices. Usually anyone can enter these races and you don't even need a racing bike.

You will swiftly gain know-how and experience, including how to warm up. It's best not to eat for at least two hours before a race, and to warm up shortly before a race begins, and to stay warmed up until it starts.

Local racing clubs offer beginning Masters racers a wealth of experience in every aspect of competition. By riding in their time trials and local races you can avoid the intense rivalry that exists in open competition. And some form of coaching may also be available.

Some local racing clubs are sponsored by local businesses that subsidize expenses, such as the cost of sending teams to distant events. In return, club members wear jerseys emblazoned with these sponsors' names.

Opportunities for Older Racers

Racing is especially rewarding for mature women because of the numerous opportunities to win top awards. During the past four decades, 27 of the individual medals won at the World's Cycling Championships were won by American women. And while the number of younger women racers tripled during the 1980s, the field in the women's Masters-50 and over remains relatively uncrowded.

If you can't find sufficiently challenging competition in your Masters age group, you are perfectly free to transfer to a lower Masters age group and to compete against younger riders. As a Masters cyclist you can also compete in races for Seniors but, naturally, you'll be riding against people aged 29 and under.

Because bike racers maintain a high level of intensity for a longer period of time than in most other sports, bike racing can be demanding, challenging, and even grueling. But in Masters racing you aren't competing in an Ironman event or in the Race Across AMerica. By setting your sights on a realistic goal, like getting top placing in a Masters competition, you can experience all the stimulation of challenge and competition without having to push yourself beyond your limits.

A Glossary of Bicycle Terms

*E*veryday terms like wheel, tire, spoke and brake, familiar to everyone who drives or owns an automobile, have been omitted. Also not included are the principal bicycle parts identified in Figures 2.1 and 2.2.

Aerobic conditioning A system of fitness-conditioning based on maintaining the heartbeat in a "target zone" for a minimum of 20 minutes at each bicycling session.

Aggressive As used in bicycling, aggressive translates into active, sporty, competitive and ready for any challenge. Hence such terms as an aggressive frame, aggressive riding, or (on a mountain bike) aggressive tires.

Alpine shifting Shifting up, step by step, from the lowest gear to the highest without missing a single gear step. To do this, several double shifts may be necessary. The gearing pattern on most touring and mountain bikes is compatible with alpine shifting. (See crossover shifting.)

ATB An all-terrain bicycle, of which there are 3 types: the mountain bicycle; the mountain racing bicycle; and the city or commuter bicycle. All use fat tires designed for off-road riding.

Bottom bracket The short round tube holding the axle between the pedals and to which both the seat tube and the down tube are attached.

Brake hoods The rubber covers which shield brake levers, allowing the hands to be placed on them while riding.

Brake lever   The "handle" or grip on the handlebar which you squeeze to apply the brake.

Butted frame   Butted means that the frame tubes are tapered so that they are slender at the middle and thicker at the ends where they enter the lugs and bear most of the stress. Butted frames are lighter and provide a livelier ride. Double, triple or quadruple butting is available. Spokes are also butted and tapered in the middle.

Cadence   Rhythm, or more specifically, the number of revolutions per minute at which the pedals are rotated. Ideally, one's cadence should range from sixty to ninety, or more, complete revolutions of the pedals per minute.

Caliper brakes   Caliper-shaped, lightweight brakes used on racing and sports bicycles. (See figure 2.3.) Though most modern caliper brakes are the sidepull type, centerpull varieties also exist.

Cantilever brakes   So-called because each brake shoe is pulled or canted inwards against the rim, these powerful centerpull brakes are widely used on touring and mountain bikes and on tandems. (See figure 2.3).

Cassette cracker   A mini-whip tool for roadside removal of most freehub cassettes. (See figure 5.4)

Century ride   An organized one-day event in which bicyclists ride individually, and at their own pace, to try and complete 100 miles in a period of 8–10 hours or less. Nowadays, a shorter metric century of 100 kilometers is also an available option.

Chainrings   Also called chainwheels, these are the toothed gears near the pedals. Racing and sports bicycles usually have two chainrings (a double crankset) while touring and mountain bikes have three (a triple crankset). (See figure 3.1).

Chainwhip   A handtool consisting of a long handle attached to a piece of chain. (See figure 5.4.) The chain is placed over the teeth of a cog that one wishes to remove or unscrew from the freewheel body or cassette. With the handle used as a lever, the cog can then be unscrewed.

Cleat   A metal or plastic slot on the sole of the shoe that engages the pedal, locking shoe and pedal together. On conventional pedals, cleats are held in place by toestraps.

Clincher tire   Similar in cross-section to an automobile tire, a clincher bicycle tire requires a separate inner tube. Almost all bicycle tires in use today are clincher tires.

Clipless pedals   A modern replacement for toeclips and straps, clip-less pedals lock the shoes to the pedals with cleats that release like a ski binding. They are also known as step-in pedals.

Cluster   The cluster of toothed gears (called cogs or sprockets) on the right side of the rear wheel of a derailleur-geared bicycle. (See figure 3.1.)

Cogs   The individual toothed gears, or sprockets, that together form a cluster on the right side of the rear wheel of a derailleur-geared bicycle.

Computer   Handlebar computers are used on bicycles to show speed, trip distance, cumulative distance, and stopwatch time. More sophisticated models show pedal cadence, heartbeat rate, and the total elevation gain of all hills climbed on the trip.

Cones   U-shaped nuts located on the axle which control the tension on wheel bearings.

Crankarm   The arm to which the pedal is attached and which transmits power to the chainrings. Crankarms are available in several different lengths.

Crankset   The assembly consisting of chainrings, axle, crankarms and pedals that rotates as a unit when you pedal.

Crossover shifting   A pattern of shifting through a bicycle's gear sequence while making only a single double shift. To accomplish this, other less useful gears that require a double shift to enter are sacrificed. The gearing on most racing and sports bicycles is compatible with crossover shifting. (See alpine shifting.)

Decals   The insignia on a bicycle, usually containing the bicycle firm's name, model, and identification of the materials used in the frame, fork and stays. Decals usually decorate all three main tubes.

Derailleur   The mechanism that actually derails the chain and moves it on to another cog or chainring. The left gearshift lever controls the front derailleur that moves the chain on to any desired chainring while the right gearshift lever controls the rear derailleur that moves the chain onto any desired cog. Derailleur shifting functions only when a bicycle is being pedaled.

Development   The development of any chainring-cog combination is a number that allows you to tell how high or low the resulting gear is and enables you to compare it with other combinations. Development tables for all gear combinations are given in Chapter 3.

Double shifting   Occurs when you must shift both front and rear derailleurs to move up or down to the next gear position in the sequence.

Draft   To ride very closely behind one or more other riders so that they partially shelter you from having to pedal against a headwind. Also known as pacing (see Paceline).

Drive train   A bicycle's entire propulsion mechanism that includes the pedals, crankarms, chainrings, cogs, derailleurs and gearshift levers — comparable to the drive train of a car. (See Figure 3.1.)

Drop-outs   U-shaped slots at the end of stays and forks into which the axles fit.

Drops   The part of the handlebar that curves downward closest to the ground. Also called hooks.

Elliptical chainrings   Chainrings that are slightly out-of-round and that, while the crankarms are vertical, ease pedaling by briefly providing the equivalent of being in a gear one step lower than the one you are actually in.

Freehub   A cassette-shaped freewheel body on to which as many as 8 cogs can be mounted. The body is shaped like the spindle of an audio cassette player, and the cogs are slipped on in a manner similar to a cassette tape.

Freewheel   The freewheel is the cluster of toothed gears on the right side of the rear wheel hub. Each individual gear of the freewheel is called a cog or sprocket and is mounted on the freewheel body. The body actually contains the pawl and rachet assembly — the true freewheel — which allows it to remain stationary while you coast, or to be rotated backwards as you backpedal.

Friction gear shifting   Shifting gears with traditional levers which depend on friction to remain in place. Since it is easy to undershift or overshift, each lever must be adjusted manually to its optimal position on the cog or chainring. (The opposite of Indexed shifting.)

Gears   The toothed cogs on the right side of the rear wheel and the toothed chainrings near the pedals. The term "gear" is also used to describe a particular chainring-cog combination. A high gear is a chainring-cog combination in which pedaling uphill is difficult while a low gear is a combination in which pedaling uphill is relatively easy.

Gearshift levers   The left gearshift lever controls the front derailleur which moves the chain onto any desired chainring, while the right gearshift lever controls the rear derailleur, which moves the chain onto any desired cog. On road bikes, the levers are usually located on the down tube or on the stem or sometimes at the handlebar tips. On mountain bikes, the left lever is on the left side of the handlebar and vice versa.

Grid chart   A small chart attached to the handlebar or handlebar bag showing the development of each chainring-cog combination.

Handlebars   Handlebars come in two basic styles: the drop-type racing style handlebar; and the flat (straight) type handlebar used on all-terrain bicycles. For those who prefer the latter, any drop-type handlebar can be replaced with a flat handlebar. New extension style handlebars that support the forearms, and that reach out over the front wheel, have become popular with racers.

Head tube angle   The angle between the top tube and the stem.

Honking   Climbing a hill while standing on the pedals — first on one pedal and then on the other — which causes the bicycle to rock from side to side. A favorite hill-climbing technique with racers, honking is also often used by touring bicyclists to climb short, steep hills without shifting down. While honking, you push a higher gear than you would do if climbing the same hill while seated.

Hub   The hub is the center piece of each wheel, into which the spokes are laced. Inside, and at each end of the hub, is a bearing that allows the hub to rotate freely on the axle.

Hyperglide shifting system   The smoothest gear shifting mechanism available, it also permits shifting cogs without having to softpedal.

Indexed gear shifting   The modern gear shifting system in which the right gearshift lever clicks you into exactly the right preset position on any desired cog. (The opposite of Friction shifting.)

Inner tube   The tubeless bicycle tire has yet to be invented and all bicycle tires still require an inner tube.

Interval training   A system of fitness-training based on pedaling intensely for a short period followed by pedaling through a slower recovery period. The cycle is repeated several times.

LSD conditioning   Stands for Long Steady Distance. A system of fitness-conditioning based on riding a moderately long distance at a steady pace.

Lugs   Lugs are used on a conventional bicycle frame to reinforce the joints formed by tubes and stays.

Mixte frame   A woman's frame in which the top tube is replaced by two stays which reach back diagonally from the top of the head tube to the rear wheel dropouts. Of French design, the mixte frame is the strongest of the frames designed for women.

Mountain bicycle   A versatile machine equipped with a wide range of gears, powerful brakes and fat tires, and designed for negotiating rough, off-road terrain and for climbing steep hills. The commonest type of all-terrain bicycle, the mountain bike is ridden in the upright position. Mountain bikes can also be fitted with road tires for travel on paved roads.

Mountain Tamer Quad   An ultra-small fourth chainring of 15T–19T that bolts on the inside of a triple crankset and provides tremendous climbing power. Currently available at mountain biking centers, the Quad is used only on mountain bikes.

Paceline   The line formed when bicyclists ride one behind the other to cut wind resistance. Each rider takes a brief spell in the lead position, then drops back to the rear of the paceline.

Panniers   Twin nylon touring bags carried on the rear wheel rack of a touring bike.

Pedals   Although pedals are familiar to almost everyone, it's important to remember that the right one has a right hand thread and the left one a left hand thread.

Presta valve   A thin, metal bicycle tube valve, the Presta holds air better than the more familiar Schrader valve that is identical to those used on automobile tires.

Quick-release axle   Quick-release axles can be secured in place, or swiftly released, by simply pressing home (or releasing) a lever on the axle of each bicycle wheel. Other quick-release levers are used on mountain bike seat posts, and to release the tension on brake cables.

Racing bicycle   A bicycle designed primarily for racing. Most racing bicycles are built for road competition (road racers), but there are also criterium racers designed for fast cornering and sprinting during criterium races. Track bicycles are another class of racing bicycle.

Rack   The metal carrier frame fitted over the rear wheel of a touring bike, on which touring bags, panniers, raingear etc., are carried. Similar front wheel racks are also used when carrying camping gear.

Recreational bicycling   This term refers specifically to non-competitive bicycling, especially to touring and mountain bicycling.

However, the term is often used interchangeably with sports bicycling.

Rim tape   An endless plastic or rubber tape that fits over the spoke heads on a bicycle wheel rim and protects the inner tube from being punctured by a protruding spoke head.

Road bicycle   A lightweight bicycle designed for use exclusively on paved roads and which uses relatively thin tires. The three principal road bike types are: racing bicycles; sports bicycles; and touring bicycles.

Saddle   The bicyclist's term for a bicycle seat.

Sealed bearings   On quality bicycles, all bearings, such as those in the wheel hubs, crankset and headset are sealed (shielded) to keep lubrication in and dirt and water out.

Seat post   The tube, or pillar, which moves up and down inside the seat tube, and which allows saddle height to be adjusted. Atop the seat post is an adjustable clamp to which the saddle is attached, and which is used to adjust saddle-tilt and fore-and-aft position.

Seat-tube angle   The angle between the seat tube and top tube.

Size, of bicycle   The size of a bicycle is determined by its frame size. Frame size is the distance between the center of the bottom bracket (or crankset axle) and the highest point on the seat tube, measured either in inches or in centimeters.

Slickrock   Areas of smooth, bare rock found in Utah and other western states, on which mountain bicycles may be ridden with minimum damage to the ecology. Around Moab, Utah, one can often ride for miles on slickrock terrain while traversing regions of majestic desert scenery.

Soft-pedaling   Easing up on pedal pressure while shifting gears, or to lose speed and slow down.

Speed   As used in the term "twelve-speed bicycle" it means that the bicycle has twelve different gear positions. In the same way, an automobile with a 4-speed transmission has four different forward gear positions.

Splines   A spline is a projection on a shaft that fits into corresponding slots on another shaft or wheel, locking both shafts so that they rotate together — as does a cassette tape when placed on the spindles of a cassette player.

Sports bicycle   A lightweight road bicycle usually equipped with two chainrings and primarily designed for club rides and day rides.

Sports bicycling   Specifically, riding a racing or sports bicycle for training or competition. The term is also often used interchangeably with Recreational bicycling.

Stay   Two sets of stays, the seat stays and chain stays, together with the seat tube, form the rear triangle of a bicycle frame.

Stem   Available with extensions of different lengths, the stem permits fine-tuning of the rider's position by allowing adjustment of the height and angle of the handlebar.

Superglide   A modern chainring shifting system that uses chainrings with uneven tooth profiles to allow the chain to glide smoothly from one chainring to another, even while climbing a hill under full load.

Toeclips   Light plastic or metal frames that hold the shoe in its correct position on the pedal. They include a strap that locks the shoe in place and that can be released by reaching down and pressing a buckle release.

Touring bicycle   A road bicycle, usually equipped with 3 chainrings and a wide range of gears, and designed to carry heavy loads on long distance tours.

True   A true (or trued) wheel is perfectly round and free of wobbles.

Tubular tire   Also called a sew-up tire. The original racing tire in which the inner tube is sewn-up inside the tube-shaped tire so that a cross section of the tire resembles that of a hosepipe. Tubular tires are attached to special wheel rims by an adhesive and can be removed in seconds.

Tuck (or tuck-in) riding position   To minimize wind resistance while coasting downhill, a bicyclist will tuck-in by crouching low over the handlebars, keeping the crankarms parallel with the road, and drawing knees and elbows in close to the body.

Wheelbase   As in an automobile, the distance between the centers of the front and rear axles.

Bicycling Organizations

Although all addresses and phone numbers were checked prior to publication, inevitably as time goes on, some addresses and phone numbers will change while some organizations may merge, change their names, or go out of existence.

American Youth Hostels (AYH)
National Office
PO Box 37613
Washington DC 20013-7613
202-783-6161

A membership organization through which members may use youth hostels worldwide, participate in local AYH bike rides, and qualify for both domestic and international bicycle tours. Write for current membership application and the *World Adventure Travel Program* brochure. Reduced membership for those 55 and over.

Bikecentennial
PO Box 8308
Missoula MT 59807
406-721-1776

The bicycle travel association, a membership organization. Write or phone for current rates. Provides complete maps to the U.S. National

Bicycle Trails Network (18,500 miles of U.S. backroads with low-volume traffic) plus the *Cyclist's Yellow Pages, Cyclosource, Bike Report* magazine and scores of other guidebooks, maps and other invaluable publications for the touring cyclist, covering both the United States and other countries. Also operates long-distance road bicycle tours plus mountain bike tours with emphasis on camping.

League of American Wheelmen
6707 Whitestone Road, Suite 209
Baltimore MD 21707
301-944-3399

A membership organization, write for current rates. As the national organization of bicyclists, the LAW maintains a strong legislative and government relations program to protect the rights and interests of bicyclists. The LAW also provides members with *Bicycle USA Almanac* and *Bicycle USA* magazine featuring all upcoming events and rallies.

National Off-Road Bicycle Association (NORBA)
1750 East Boulder Street
Colorado Springs CO 80909
303-578-4581

As the national governing body for mountain bicycle racing, NORBA issues mountain bicycle racing licenses.

Tandem Club of America
c/o Mac & Jean Smith
11010 Jamison Road
East Aurora NY 14052
716-652-4765

A membership club for tandem owners and riders; write for current membership rate. Members receive a newsletter announcing all tandem events and rallies.

U.S. Cycling Federation, Inc. (USCF)
1750 East Boulder Street
Colorado Springs CO 80909
303-578-4581

The national governing body for amateur competitive cycling in the United States. Issues licenses for road and track racing.

Women's Cycling Network
Box 73
Harvard IL 60033

A membership source for all women's events, tours, workshops, and hospitality homes.

Publishers and Publications

Backcountry Publications
A division of The Countryman Press, Inc. (see below)

Bicycle Guide
711 Boylston Street
Boston MA 02116
617-236-1885

A monthly magazine specializing in in-depth reviews of bicycles and cycling techniques.

Bicycling Magazine
33 East Minor Street
Emmaus PA 18098
215-967-5171

The largest U.S. monthly bicycling magazine. For mountain bike enthusiasts, *Bicycling* publishes with each issue a special version, *Bicycling plus Mountain Bike,* which includes an extra section on mountain bicycling.

The Countryman Press, Inc.
(includes Backcountry Publications)
P.O. Box 175
Woodstock VT 05091
802-457-1049

Offers bicycle touring guides to the Northeast, Mid-Atlantic, and some midwestern states, plus books on bicycle racing and training. Write for free catalog.

Fat Tire Flyer
Box 757
Fairfax CA 94930
415-457-7016

A bimonthly magazine devoted to mountain bicycling.

The Globe Pequot Press
P.O. Box Q
Chester CT 06412
203-526-957!

Publishes bicycle touring guides to the Northeast and mid-Atlantic states. Write for free catalog.

Velo-News
5595 Arapahoe Avenue, Suite G
Boulder CO 80303
303-440-0601

The journal of competitive bicycling. Also available are books on training and racing.

Vitesse Press
Box 1886
Brattleboro VT 05301-1886
802-254-2305

Publishes books on bicycle racing and training.

Map Sources

Michelin Maps & Guides
PO Box 3305
Spartanburg SC 29304
1-800-423-0485

Publishes detailed road maps of France, Benelux, Portugal, Spain, Switzerland, Greece, Yugoslavia, Denmark, and Morocco. Write for map and price list.

Distribution Branch
U.S. Geological Survey
Box 25286
Federal Center, Building 4
Denver CO 80225
303-236-7477

U.S. Geological Survey topographical maps of the United States. Name states for which you require map indexes (free).

Bicycle Equipment Catalogs

Aerobic Fitness Group
5948 Pleasanton Avenue
Minneapolis MN 55419
1-800-654-3670

    Free catalog of bicycles and equipment.

Bike Nashbar
P.O. Box 3449
Youngstown OH 44513–3449
1-800-627-4227

    Write for extensive mailorder catalog of bicycles and equipment.

Cycle Goods
2801 Hennepin Avenue South
Minneapolis MN 55408
1-800-328-5213

    Write or phone for extensive mailorder catalog of bicycles and equipment.

Performance Bicycle Shop
Box 2741
Chapel Hill NC 27514
1-800-727-2453

    Write or phone for free mailorder bicycle equipment catalog.

REI
PO Box 88125
Seattle WA 98138
1-800-426-4840

    Write for *Cyclosource* mailorder catalog of bicycles and equipment. REI was originally called Recreational Equipment International.

INDEX

Bicycling Books Available from
The Countryman Press

The Countryman Press and its associated companies, long known for fine books on outdoor recreation, offer a range of practical and readable books on bicycling.

Bicycle Touring Books from Backcountry Publications

25 Bicycle Tours on Delmarva, by John R. Wennersten, $8.95
25 Bicycle Tours in Eastern Pennsylvania, by Dale Adams and Dale Speicher, $8.95
20 Bicycle Tours in the Finger Lakes, by Mark Roth and Sally Walters, $8.95
20 Bicycle Tours in the Five Boroughs (NYC), by Sandy Wolferman, $8.95
25 Bicycle Tours in the Hudson Valley, by Howard Stone, $9.95
25 Bicycle Tours in Maine, by Howard Stone, $9.95
25 Bicycle Tours in New Hampshire, by Tom and Susan Heavey, $7.95
25 Bicycle Tours in New Jersey, by Arline Zatz and Joel Zatz, $8.95
20 Bicycle Tours in and around New York City, by Dan Carlinsky and David Heim, $7.95
25 Bicycle Tours in Ohio's Western Reserve, by Sally Walters, $9.95
25 Bicycle Tours in Vermont, by John Freidin, $8.95
25 Mountain Bike Tours in Vermont, by William J. Busha, $9.95
Backcountry Publications offers many more books on canoeing, fishing, hiking, walking, and ski touring in New England, New York State, the Mid-Atlantic States, and the Midwest.

Bicycling and Bicycle Racing Books from Vitesse Press

Beginning Bicycle Racing, by Fred Matheny, $14.95
Fit and Fast: How to Be a Better Cyclist, by Karen Roy and Thurlow Rogers, $15.95
Pedaling Across America, by Don and Lolly Skillman, $9.95
Tales from the Bike Shop, by Maynard Hershon, $13.95

Our titles are available in bookshops and in many sporting goods stores, or they may be ordered directly from the publisher. When ordering by mail, please add $2.50 per order for shipping and handling. To order or obtain a complete catalog, please write The Countryman Press, Inc., P.O. Box 175, Woodstock, Vermont 05091.

7504   3991